Street Crazy

Bill DiMonda

PublishAmerica
Baltimore

First printing

ISBN: 1-4241-6202-5
PUBLISHED BY PUBLISHAMERICA, LLLP
www.publishamerica.com
Baltimore

Printed in the United States of America

This book is dedicated with love
to my wife and six children,
all of whom have given me
the support and courage
to finish my work.

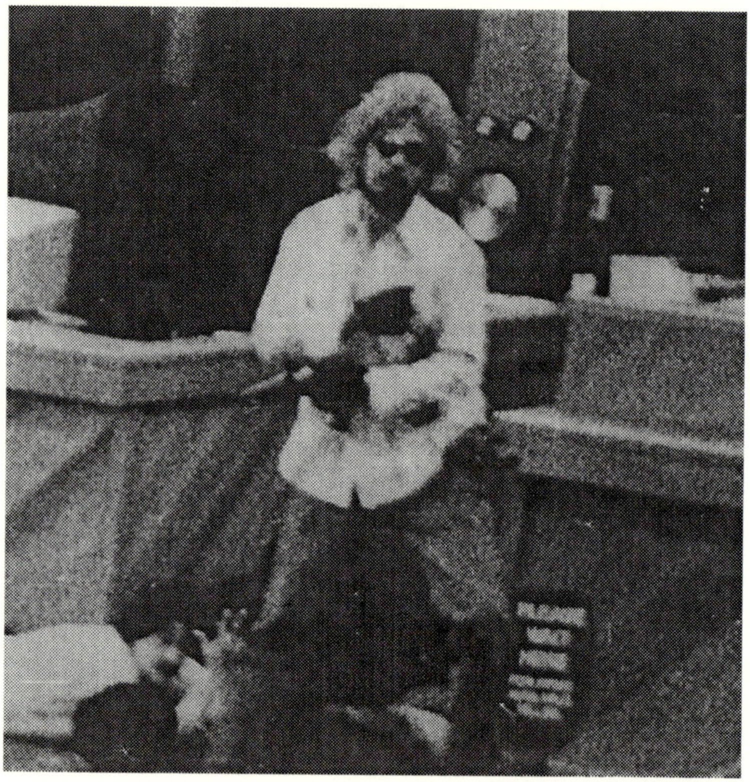

During the 1930s, John Dillinger, America's number-one desperado, captured the attention of citizens and law enforcement officers alike. This notorious bank robber's tools of the trade were a Thompson sub-machine gun and a revolver. Although admired by many for his daring and cast as a folk hero, Dillinger gunned down ten men. "Pretty Boy" Floyd began his criminal career by robbing a local post office of $350 in pennies. Like Dillinger, he killed ten people. Who can forget the murder and robbery spree of Bonnie Parker and Clyde Barrow through Missouri, Texas and Oklahoma?

The preceding is a vivid example of the violent nature of many robberies. Robbery is one of the three most violent crimes against the person. Only homicide and rape are considered to be more traumatic to the victim. (Wayne W. Bennett, Karen M. Hess, *Criminal Investigations,* 339, 5th ed., 1998.)

Prologue

He stood at an open window in the daylight basement of the house and stared out at the quiet little suburb. The row of split-level homes, each with its manicured front lawn and cement sidewalk, could not be distinguished from any of the other small communities that had sprung up in the suburbs north of Seattle in the past year or two. As he watched the neighborhood children play and listened to their laughter, something bothered him, but he couldn't quite put a finger on it. He stood wondering, as his hand drifted automatically to the pack of Winston cigarettes in his shirt pocket. Nervously he selected a cigarette and lit it.

The radio was blaring out Perry Como's original rendition of "Seattle" as he impatiently inhaled, waiting for the news broadcast. It was almost 5:00 p.m. and still he hadn't heard any news about the robbery. When the song ended the disc jockey switched gears and headed straight into the hourly news broadcast.

He listened intently as the day's events were rehashed. When the news ended he walked slowly across the room to the small radio and turned it off. Why hadn't it been mentioned? Surely a bank robbery in broad daylight would be news. Everyone of the group aside from the redhead and her boyfriend had returned. What happened to them? He felt uneasy as he sat on the sofa and pondered what to do next. As he reached for another cigarette his instincts told him it was time to leave. But how could he? For the first time in his life he was torn between his basic instinct of survival and loyalty to a woman. Unable to clear his thoughts, he put his head down on the sofa and drifted toward sleep.

Just then the phone upstairs rang!

"It's for you," a scratchy voice yelled down the staircase from the kitchen above.

He sprang from his chair and hurtled, two steps at a time, up the carpeted stairway of the split-level home. When he reached the phone he was out of breath and was forced to stop and take a deep breath before he could talk.

"Yeah?" After a few seconds he added, "I was hoping it would be you. Is everything alright? You have the stuff?" Nodding his head as the caller spoke, he replied, "Where should I meet you? What time?" He paused and thought for a moment. "No, let's meet somewhere else; too many cops up there. Hold on." He placed his hand over the receiver and turned to the bearded man who had just entered the room. "Where's a safe place up on Aurora that you know of?"

Without hesitation the bearded man answered, "'Frank's on 50th and Aurora."

He returned his attention to the phone and said, "You know where Frank's on 50th and Aurora is?" He waited for the reply then finished, "I'll be there, just make sure that you are."

He hung up the phone and walked back downstairs. Looking around at the contents of the room, he knew he couldn't afford to leave all this, yet he must. He reasoned to himself that it would only be for a few hours. Just enough time to meet his brother-in-law, maybe score a little heroin and hopefully find out what the hell was going on. He placed another cigarette in his mouth and lit it. Now the feelings of paranoia began to resurface. Was there anyone that he could trust? Of course not!

Not even family. Walking over to a small wooden dresser on the far wall, he opened the top draw and removed a 25-caliber automatic. After checking to see that the clip was fully loaded, he racked one round into the chamber, checked the safety and tucked the gun into the waistband of his jeans, pulling out his shirt to cover it.

Shortly before 6:00 p.m., a green two-door Oldsmobile hard-top backed out of a driveway in the quiet residential area north of the King County line, and proceeded towards its destiny. The next few hours would decide if the Northwest's longest and most brutal crime sprees in recent history would continue or come to an untimely end.

Chapter 1

Because it is situated between the Pacific Ocean and the Cascade Mountains, Seattle tends to receive more than its share of moisture year round. Winters, although relatively mild, are wet and green. Perched atop Seattle's Space Needle it was easy to see why many of the city's inhabitants believed this was God's country. The view was nothing less than magnificent: Mounts Rainier, Adams and Hood to the south; Mount Baker and the Canadian Rockies to the north; the Cascade Mountains to the east and the spectacular Olympic Peninsula with its majestic mountain range and lush rain forest to the west. Tiny wisps of smoke snaked up from the chimneys of homes wedged between the rich landscape of firs and cedars, giving the city an almost fairytale-like setting.

It was mid-December, and a light mist fell over the city. The temperature had dropped to the mid-forties and the dampness penetrated the thick concrete walls that enclosed the County Court House, a twelve-story stone and concrete structure located in downtown Seattle on 3rd and James Streets. The building housed the King County Executive's office, the Department of Public Safety and its communication center, the King County Superior Courts and the overcrowded, undermanned King County Jail, which encompassed most of its top three floors.

On the twelfth floor, a lone figure, slightly slumped at the shoulders, stood, eyes straining, as he tried to view the cars and the rain-soaked people through the thick plexiglas and wire meshed windows that framed his home above the street. How long had it been now? The year and a half that he spent in this jail facility was slipping by, numbed by the effect of a self-induced drug euphoria, which, even now seemed to linger on. He knew the reason he was behind bars today was his uncontrollable addiction to heroin. With the thought of this fatal mistake firmly imprinted on his mind, he turned his attention to the matter at hand.

He was certainly no stranger to this type of life, having bounced in and out of juvenile homes, county and local jails as well as state prison since his adolescent years. In fact, he felt almost comfortable in this type of controlled environment.

At thirty-eight, Johnny Hardy was not just your run-of-the-mill two-bit punk down on his luck. He was one of the "new breed" of criminals who relentlessly prowled our urban streets in constant search of a helpless victim. He was known by his friends (whatever few he had) and associates to possess the qualities which so often brought out the animal instincts man developed eons before, and which, for most of us, are currently buried deep within our subconscious. Johnny Hardy was a survivor, driven solely by his desire to be free. Word on the street, where Johnny made his living, was that he was crazy. No, not crazy in the way you and I, or even *Webster's Collegiate Dictionary* define it. In reality it was more appropriate to label Hardy as "street crazy." This unusual label was given to those individuals who would do anything or commit any crime for any reason they perceived necessary, for their own survival. For this reason, Hardy had become, among his peers, one of the most respected and feared figures in the criminal element of the Northwest.

Just then the jail intercom blared, clearing out the cobwebs in his head, and announced the end of his workout period. Turning slowly, Hardy deliberately shuffled across the worn wooden floor of the workout area toward the unlocked gate leading back to the cellblocks. From that gate he walked down a narrow passageway to his temporary home on C deck (one of three decks that comprised the King County Jail). As he reached his destination an officer waiting at the other end of the cell block outside the gate withdrew a large key from his key ring and opened the "lock box," a solid steel box approximately three feet high and two feet wide hanging next to his work station. Once the box was opened the officer manually depressed a lever and the thick steel bars blocking the entranceway to the cellblock area rattled noisily back along its track to allow entrance to his home within. He shuffled down the long corridor that ran in a U-shaped pattern around the outside of twenty individual cells within the cellblock. When he reached his cell, the officer depressed another lever, releasing his individual cell door. He walked in and with a small sigh sat on his bunk and awaited his meeting with fate, just a few short hours away.

Shortly after 1:00 p.m. that afternoon the officer on duty repeated the same process and the steel door to Hardy's cell slid open. By the time the door was opened, two jail guards appeared to escort him from his tiny four-man cell, which now housed five inmates, to his final court appearance. Hardy, clad only in his jail slippers and red jail-issued coverall, rolled down from his bunk and headed out the door. The two officers dressed in their tan uniforms with county jail patches on their left shoulders led him down the corridor of the poorly ventilated living quarters through the cellblock entrance and then walked behind him as he shuffled down the long cement ramps that led through the three floors of the jail to the main booking area. C deck, where Johnny had spent the last eighteen months, housed the hard-timers. These were inmates who were doing at least one year of county time, were waiting to be transferred to a state prison or were considered a security risk. B deck, one floor below, housed the habitual, but not necessarily violent, repeat offenders and A deck was primarily the intake deck for new prisoners, crazies, drunks and prisoners that posed a minimal security threat.

As he shuffled down the last ramp toward the main desk area of the jail, he recognized the familiar sound of spray guns used to delouse the new inmates. Whenever there was an unusual influx of new prisoners, the distinctive foul odor of the lice spray would seep up through the decks and sicken many of the inmates on both decks above. The smell had really never bothered him since he had long ago learned to live with the stench that permeated the entire three floors of the jail.

Within minutes, he stood before a wall of solid steel bars fifteen feet high, which separated the jail's living quarters from the main booking area. In the corner of the booking area stood the "pill box," a cement bunker much like those you would see in a B-grade WWII movie. Only this one was fronted with one-way bulletproof glass so that the jail personnel inside could view the entire booking area while being assured of their own anonymity as well as safety within. Inside, the assigned officer controlled power to all of the cellblocks within the jail, the booking area, all the gates between the cellblocks and the booking area, and all the entrance and exit doors to the jail facility. Not long ago you could find the door to the control room open through most of the day, allowing access to anyone who happened to be in the booking area at the time. It had taken a daring daytime escape attempt to correct that bit of carelessness in the procedures. Hardy knew there would be no second chances for that type of mistake. His only chance now lay in the preparations he had made prior to his arrest.

The electronic lock on the gate snapped open and with one officer ahead and one behind, he was ushered through the gate and into a six-by-six cage used as a temporary holding cell for inmates being transported to court proceedings.

While he sat and stared at his surroundings, he bummed a cigarette from another inmate in the cell. Meanwhile, the two officers who escorted him prepared the necessary paperwork and collected their black web belts and empty holsters from a small room adjacent to the booking area. When the paperwork was done and their belts and holsters placed firmly around their waists, the older of the two guards opened the holding cell door and motioned for Hardy to come out. He casually pushed himself up from the hard wooden bench and took the last drag off his cigarette before he crushed it under his foot. Then he strolled casually out of the cage as if he were simply walking down the street. Only this time as he crossed the threshold of the cage he was instantly jolted back into reality by the younger of the two guards who had reached out, grabbed him by the arm and instantly spun him around against the steel bars of the holding cell.

"You know the drill, asshole. Spread 'em."

"Say, man, it's not necessary..." But before he could finish, the hard fiberglass point of the officer's nightstick found its mark between two of his lower ribs. The blow, although not hard, caught him off-guard. A sharp pain shot through his entire body and he doubled over trying to catch his breath. When he finally regained his breath, he reluctantly reached out and grabbed one bar with each hand, spread his legs and extended his long sinewy six-foot frame for a routine pat-down. When the pat-down was completed, both hands were handcuffed securely behind his back. He was led to a solid-core steel door which opened with a loud click to the confines of a small caged area surrounding the two elevators that led down to the courtrooms below. Once inside the cage, with the door secured firmly behind them, both officers opened small wall lockers adjacent to the bank of elevators, removed their loaded firearms, and placed them in the holsters on their belts. A bell sounded and the elevator doors opened. Within a few seconds all three men disappeared into the bowels of the courthouse.

Chapter 2

It is extremely difficult, unless you travel the hallways of the courthouse daily, to tell one floor from another. Since the officer in the control booth controlled the destination of the elevator, it was impossible for Hardy to know with any certainty what floor he and the officers had exited on. As the three men stepped out into the hallway, they immediately headed for the east wing of the courthouse where his sentencing would take place.

The noise from prosecutors, defense attorneys and defendants ended abruptly as the solid oak double doors opened and Hardy and his entourage entered the courtroom. In the center of the enormous oak-trimmed courtroom a plain eight-foot wood-grained table sat on the cold and dirty tile floor. On the right side of the table in two wooden office chairs the prosecutor and his assistant sat busily reviewing the last-minute changes in the court calendar. On the other side, in a similarly worn wooden armchair, Hardy's court-appointed attorney-dressed in a wrinkled blue polyester suit, waited patiently for the third of his eight scheduled court appearances that day.

Hardy approached the table and stood next to his attorney. With his arrival, the bailiff quickly notified the judge waiting in his chambers. The guards removed the handcuffs and Hardy sat down, rubbing his chafed wrists.

"All rise. The Honorable Judge John Callahan now presiding."

Callahan, the oldest superior court justice in King County, entered the room. At age sixty-six, dressed in the traditional black robe covering black slacks and a white shirt and tie, Callahan appeared to be a man twenty years his junior. Tall and slender, with light brown curly hair, sporting a neatly trimmed golden brown beard spotted here and there with patches of gray, Callahan gave the appearance of a movie star, rather than a magistrate conducting a court proceeding. He scanned the courtroom, took his seat behind the bench and began.

"Please be seated." Looking down from his perch he announced, "This is the case of *State vs. Hardy*." Shifting his eyes to the attorneys seated at the table he continued, "Are both counsels prepared to proceed?"

The prosecutor and the defense attorney acknowledged the question and he proceeded.

"I have read all the court files and documents concerning this matter, including probation reports and the briefs that both the prosecutor and the client's attorney have submitted." Once again directing his attention to the attorneys he said, "Before I continue with sentencing, do either of you have anything else to add?"

"Nothing else, your honor," replied the prosecutor.

"May I have one moment to speak with my client, your honor?" Hardy's attorney turned and spoke quietly to him. After a moment, it was evident that Hardy had nothing else to add to the proceedings and his attorney replied, "Nothing more, your honor."

Hardy showed no visible signs of emotion as Judge Callahan sentenced him to twenty years in the state penitentiary. He fought to focus his attention on his desire to be free. And that desire didn't include twenty years behind bars.

When the proceeding was completed, Hardy knew the drill. He pushed back his chair, stood up at the desk and waited for the two officers that had escorted him earlier. As they approached, one of the officers removed the handcuffs from the pouch on his belt. Without a word, Hardy placed his hands behind his back and the cuffs were fastened securely. As the two officers led Hardy toward the courtroom exit, he glanced to the back row of the courtroom. There, almost unnoticed, sitting quietly in the last row, was a young woman in her late twenties. She had long black hair braided neatly behind her head, and she wore a black leather jacket, white silk blouse and black jeans. She sat there perfectly still, staring at the three men as they exited the room. Neither his nod nor faint smile directed at the young woman was detected by anyone else in the courtroom. But he knew his message had been received.

Chapter 3

The alarm rang as Nora Chin, her sleek naked body sandwiched between the sheets of the queen-sized sleeper, struggled to pull herself from a deep sleep. She was becoming accustomed to sleeping alone these days, but that would soon change. She swung her feet off the sofa bed and onto the cold hardwood floor of the one-bedroom apartment she had occupied since Johnny's arrest eighteen month ago. She reached over and grabbed a picture of her and Johnny that was on the end table next to the sofa. Her sister had taken it almost two years ago on a camping trip they had taken in eastern Washington. As she looked at the picture, the thought of him being led from the courtroom just a few short days before flashed through her brain. She saw that flicker in his eyes and that faint smile on his lips as he was led out the door. He would be back soon. She would help see to that. She took a moment to go over in her head all of the details they had discussed before he was arrested. Would he remember everything? She worried for a minute. Johnny always told her she worried too much. It was just up to her to take care of her part of the plan, and he would take care of the rest.

She looked at the clock. It was 10:30 a.m., and already she had let too much of the morning slip away. She replaced the photograph and pushed her tired body from the bed. Reaching for her robe she headed for the kitchen to make herself a cup of coffee. While waiting for her coffee to brew, she took a pencil from the cupboard and carefully made several lists of the things she had do that day. As soon as the coffee brewed, she grabbed a clean cup from the sink, poured herself a hot cup and quickly scurried into the bathroom. Stripping the robe from her body, she stared into the full-length mirror attached to the back of the bathroom door. At twenty-nine she was extremely proud of her body. She gazed into the mirror and stared at her firm breasts, shapely hips and tight butt. How wonderful it felt to be attractive to men. But how long would that last? She held out her arms in disbelief. Once tender and soft, they were now ravaged by the scars of her addiction. How long would it be until the rest of her body followed? What was even worse, her addiction was costing her over six hundred dollars a week and numerous scrapes with the law. Since Johnny was gone she was forced to supply her habit with the profits she made from shoplifting expensive items and returning them for cash or selling them outright on the street. (The latter was always the last resort, since selling them on the street only brought about ten cents on the dollar.) Although a profitable business venture, the risks she ran due to improved store security were extremely high. In the past six months she had been arrested at three different department stores. Each time she was arrested, she produced phony identification Johnny had provided for her before his arrest. Since the phony identification provided her with a clean background, she was cited by the police and released from custody to go on her merry way to yet another store.

She turned on the shower and while waiting for the water to heat up, pinned her braided hair on top of her head. Stepping into the shower, she washed quickly. When she finished, she wiped dry with a plush light blue terrycloth towel, compliments of the downtown Nordstrom store, wrapped the towel around her waist and then went back to the front room of the apartment where her clothes were draped over a worn leather armchair. Letting the towel fall to the floor and sitting on the arm of the chair, she finished the cup of coffee she had poured for herself. She loved to hang out in the apartment naked. In fact, in the last eighteen months, she had become somewhat of an exhibitionist, sometimes leaving her living room curtains open, allowing a teenage boy in the complex across the street to view her in all stages of undress. But this morning she had little time for excitement. She quickly slipped into a pair of satin panties with matching bra. "Thank you, Bon Marche," she mused to herself as she pulled on a pair of jeans and black sweatshirt. While she knelt to tie her running shoes, she remembered the lists she had written. Walking into the kitchen, she picked up the lists from the counter, placed them in an envelope, tucked the envelope in her black leather purse and headed out the door.

Chapter 4

This place was driving him crazy. Sitting in his cell, the furrows of his brow creased in thought, Johnny knew that if it weren't for his obsessive desire to be free and his confidence to survive, he could not have made it this long. It was torturous but necessary to dry out and temporarily withdraw from his heroin addiction, while, at the same time, his worsening physical condition, brought about by his own means, had gotten to the point that he could no longer continue without medical care. Meanwhile, his legal tactics progressed as planned. He fired his first court-appointed attorney on the grounds that the attorney was incompetent and had not defended him in a manner that would have given him a fair and adequate opportunity to prove himself not guilty. He demanded that the court appoint another attorney to review his allegations. At the same time he filed an appeal requesting that the verdict of his trial be overturned and he be freed on bail pending the new trial. Johnny wasn't stupid. He knew he didn't have one chance in hell of this happening. He was taking a calculated risk (and a good one at that) that all the additional court actions and pending actions would ultimately delay his transfer from the county jail facility to the undesirable location of the state prison east of the mountains in the city of

Walla Walla. If he could accomplish this, and he had no doubt that he could, he knew his plan would succeed.

Now, as he sat waiting patiently for the wheels of justice to come to a screeching halt, his mind drifted back to the last time he had seen Nora. She entered the visiting room and sat across from him on the other side of the glass partition. He was very impressed at how much she had learned from him in the short time they had been together. Picking up the phone on his side of the partition he spoke, "Hello, babe. You look terrific!" He always knew she had special talents, but not necessarily out of bed. This proved to him that maybe there was a little more to this woman than he thought. Johnny was known to many of his associates as the man of a thousand faces. So good was his ability to change his appearance that some nicknamed him the chameleon. Now he was pleasantly surprised to see that some of that ability had rubbed off on her.

Looking up from behind her dark-tinted cool-ray sunglasses, she smiled. She wore a pair of faded denim jeans with an open blue jean shirt over a white tube top that compressed her large breasts so tightly that she appeared to have very little chest at all. On her head she wore a brown wig that flowed down over her shoulders and completely covered the ebony braids she had so deftly tucked underneath.

"Well, what do you think?" she said while removing her sunglasses and revealing the newly acquired colored contact lenses.

Amazed at her uncanny ability, he was speechless for a moment. "Unbelievable. Just unbelievable. Now let's hope you fool everyone else. Did you use the ID I got for you to get in here today?" She nodded. "It's been hell all these months not seeing you, but I think it was the safest thing to do. Everything depends on the fact that no one can identify who you are, especially during the initial stages of the plan. Have you been staying out of trouble?"

She lied and then changed the subject. "Do you remember everything we set up?"

"Do I remember? You're damn right I remember. You just make sure everything I told you to do is done on time. Do YOU understand?"

She nodded her head meekly, remembering the ill-gotten temper Johnny had at times. Submissively she said, "I've remembered everything. And it will all be taken care of when the time comes."

"The time has come, baby. Do everything exactly as I've told you. Don't fuck up and don't do anything to draw attention to you. Do you understand? We'll only have one shot at this and it's got to be done right."

Shifting restlessly in her seat, she smiled reassuringly, but couldn't help but think about the little shoplifting excursions that she and her sister had been on lately. Momentarily daydreaming, she was jarred back to reality as he said, "That number I gave you in the north end. It's a friend. Any trouble at all and you call that number and tell them who you are. They'll get someone to help you right away. Do you understand?"

She shook her head in acknowledgment and said, "I've missed you so much. Should I come again tomorrow?"

"No!" he said a little more harshly than he should have. He quickly regained his composure, smiled at her and continued. "By next week this town will be history for both of us. They've already arranged for my doctor visit for late next week. I've got someone in the infirmary. He'll let me know as soon as they get the date up there. I'll call you as soon as I know. It may be short notice, so make sure everything is ready." He paused and placed his outstretched hand on the glass. She did the same. "Don't be frightened, it will all be over soon."

Chapter 5

As she backed the van from the parking stall, the first thing she did was scan the area in the parking lot to make sure no one was following her. It was unlikely the police were aware of any of the upcoming events or even had any idea she was connected with Johnny in any way. But, he had told her, it never hurts to be sure. As she drove out of the apartment parking lot, the van turned south on Delridge Way. After three blocks, she turned west on SW Barton, drove a short distance and made a quick right on 23rd Avenue SW, where she pulled over. When she was sure that no one was following her she continued northbound on 23rd and wound through the Highpoint and Delridge areas of south Seattle until she reached Fauntleroy Way SE. From Fauntleroy she drove across the West Seattle Bridge and went northbound on Interstate 5. As she passed through the heart of downtown Seattle, she caught a glimpse of the city's most famous landmark, the Space Needle. Built in 1962 for the World's Fair hosted by the city, this gigantic monolith was now part of the Seattle Center complex which had since been converted into a year-round cultural and amusement center. Millions of visitors of all ages visit the seventy-four-acre site which consists of the Fun Forest Amusement Park, the

Children's Museum, the Seattle Children's Theater, the Pacific Science Center and a host of other attractions.

She checked her watch. It was 11:15. She still had three hours before she had to be at the center. She continued on Interstate 5 across the Ship Canal Bridge and northbound past the University district where the state's largest and most prestigious university, the University of Washington, was located. The university, founded in 1861, was little more than a backwoods school until 1909 when it became the focus of national attention as the site of the 1909 World's Fair called the Alaska-Yukon-Pacific Exposition.

She continued northbound continually scanning her rear view mirror for anything remotely suspicious. The sky was clear and the air was crisp and cold as she drove along the three-lane freeway looking for her first stop. As she approached the exit for 1st Avenue NE, she merged into the right lane and exited the freeway adjacent to the Northgate Mall. After a left turn off the exit ramp and a quick right turn on Northgate Way, she pulled into the parking lot at the north end of the mall, parked in front of the Rainier Bank, and went inside. She could feel her heart pounding in her chest as though it were ready to explode as she went through the door and up to the customer service counter where she waited for the service teller to finish with her last customer. Finally it was her turn. She filled out a form on a small pad and handed it to the teller. While the teller walked over to a bank of drawers on the opposite side of the customer service counter to verify the signature card on file at the bank, Nora fidgeted nervously with her keys. She returned in just a minute and led Nora behind the counter and into a vault containing hundreds of safety deposit boxes. Nora removed a key from her purse and gave it to the teller who placed it into one of the dual locks on box number 125. Then the teller placed a matching bank key into the second lock and removed the box from its home in the wall. Taking it to a secure room adjacent to the vault, Nora removed several pieces of gold jewelry left over from a jewelry store robbery they had done several years before. Underneath the jewelry she found a legal-size manila envelope that Johnny had sealed and placed into the box months before his arrest. Since she never entered the box after they rented it, she was not aware of any of its contents, other than the jewelry. That is, until now. She removed the envelope and broke the seal. Inside the envelope was a set of seven white business-size envelopes, each sealed with tape. As she opened each envelope, the expression on her face turned from sheer disbelief to total anger. Inside each envelope wrapped neatly together with a rubber band was a bundle of thirty $100 bills. For the past year and a half she had been living in that dump they called an apartment barely getting by with what she could steal, risking going to jail just to get enough for another fix. That son-of-a-bitch let her struggle knowing that all he had to do was tell her about this!

It took her a few moments to collect herself, but when she did, she realized just why he hadn't told her about the money. It was obvious, of course. She would have shot it up her arms, devouring it in no time, leaving her in the same position she was in now and worse. Because without this money, he would be left to rot in jail for the next twenty years and she would be left without him; definitely her loss as well as his. He knew her well, maybe even better than she knew herself. She realized that once again he had done what, in the long run, would be best for both of them. She hurriedly stashed the bills back in the envelope and tucked it into the large shoulder bag she was carrying. Then placing the jewelry back in the box, she returned the box to its place in the wall and walked out of the vault.

She returned to the van and headed northbound on the freeway once again. This time she didn't exit until she was well out of the Seattle city limits. He had instructed her to go to Everett, a sprawling port town some thirty miles north of Seattle, a port once known for its lumber and pulp mills. It was now the county seat of Snohomish County and the western terminus of the western segment of U.S. Highway 2. It was also known as the home to the largest building in the world by volume at 116.5 million cubic feet (13.3 million cubic meters), Boeing's assembly plant for the 747 and its other huge aircraft.

When she reached Everett, she turned off the freeway and followed the directions he had mapped out. She drove directly to a little travel agency just north of the city jail on Broadway and purchased two airline tickets. By the time she finished purchasing the tickets it was one o'clock. She still had over an hour before her rendezvous, so she decided to stop at McDonald's for lunch. After a quick hamburger, fries and shake she was back on Interstate 5 heading southbound out of Everett for Seattle once again. At about 1:55 that afternoon, she exited the freeway at Mercer Street and wound around the south end of Lake Union across Broad Street to Fifth Avenue where she parked in a parking lot on Harrison and 5th across from Memorial Stadium and the Seattle Center.

For Nora, a girl motivated by physical lusts and adventure, her entrance into the Seattle Center through a short narrow alley next to the amusement center for a semi-clandestine rendezvous with a friend of Johnny's she had never met, was like entering into the world of a James Bond movie. Her entire body tingled in anticipation and an uncontrollable urge for passion overwhelmed her.

She walked west through the Center grounds to the International Fountain situated between the Coliseum and the Center House. During the spring and summer months, the fountain, which contained a number of fountainheads in its base, would resound with classical music timed to the gushing of individual fountainheads. A favorite with the children, the fountain was normally packed with kids of all ages who were soaked from head to toe in their attempts to evade the jetting fountains. Nora took a seat on one of the large stone benches that encircled the fountain, close to the Flag Plaza. She sat there almost fifteen minutes, and was about to leave when a bright-eyed, red-cheeked little boy about ten years old, in blue jeans and a red wool jacket, suddenly appeared and blocked her way.

"Hi ,lady," he shouted, startling her. "Your boyfriend said to meet him in there," pointing toward the Center House with a short stubby finger. "He said he'd meet you at the Orange Julius in a few minutes." Nora sat puzzled for a moment trying to take in the meaning of the child's words. Suddenly, the realization of what he said shot a rush of adrenaline through her body. She sprang from the hard stone bench and bounded across the open plaza toward the doorway on the west side of the Center House. (The Center House featured many ethnic festivals and a food court where one could pick up lunch and stroll outside to dine leisurely.) She pulled open the heavy steel door and entered a hallway that led to a large laminated wood floor, similar to a gym. Outlining this enormous area in the center of the building was a potpourri of fast food franchises. She quickly located the Orange Julius store on the far side of the complex and darted across the floor to the crowded counter. She stopped about twenty yards from the front counter and cautiously scanned the hundreds of people milling in the area. Johnny did not tell her anything about the appearance of the man she would meet, but she assumed it would be someone that she already knew. When she didn't recognize anyone, she took her place in line behind a young blond woman and her two whining children. When she reached the counter, she ordered a drink and reached into her purse for money to pay.

"No need for that," a voice resonated over her shoulder.

As she turned, a man much larger than the voice had intimated stared down at her. Removing a hand from his pants pocket, he placed several dollars on the counter and then, firmly gripping Nora by the hand, led her to a table close by. When they were seated, Nora noticed that this man, whoever he was, was a man unaccustomed to physical labor. His hands were large but silky soft without a callus. His fingernails were neatly trimmed and manicured, his hair coifed and his clothes immaculate. *Who is this man?* she thought.

As if reading her mind he said, "Allow me to introduce myself." Although he had a thick Spanish accent, she immediately picked up East Coast from the way he pronounced his words.

"I am Lorenzo Pena. Johnny once described you to me over the phone, but I must say that even he could not do you justice." Pena, a real slick operator from New Jersey, spent over a year with Hardy while in the joint in New York. Not only had Hardy taught him everything he knew, but he once saved his life when some members of a rival faction had cornered him alone one evening in the workout yard. If it weren't for Hardy's quick thinking, right now he would be nothing more than a few lines on a prison graveyard headstone. He owed a lot to Johnny, and he had a feeling Johnny was about to cash in some of those chips. "I owe him much, now he writes me and says he needs my help, so I come. What can I do for him…and you?"

Nora was still awestruck by the good looks of the man seated in front of her. She placed her purse on the table between them, opened it and reached in to retrieve one of the lists that she had prepared that morning. Instinctively, two men sitting at a table next to theirs reached inside their jackets. Pena, noticeably annoyed, turned toward both men, said something in Spanish and dismissed them. As they got up and left the area, Pena turned back to Nora and apologized. "Regretfully, Senorita, sometimes my associates are a little overprotective. Please forgive them." Nora nodded and then removed the list from her purse and handed it to Pena who carefully opened the folded paper. Without the slightest trace of surprise, he finished reading the list, smiled and looked across at Nora.

"My brother asks for very few favors, but when he does ask, he does not fool around." He thought for a moment then asked, "So when will you need these things?"

Nora explained to him that Johnny would be contacting her within the week to let her know when. "How long will it take you to get them when I call you?" His intense stare caused a tingle of excitement to return to her body.

"For Johnny, and of course you, my pretty lady, these items are just a phone call away. When you decide you need them," he took a pen from his pocket and scribbled a phone number on a napkin, "you call this number, day or night. Within two hours you will have what you need." With that, he reached across the table, held her chin in the fingertips of his massive hand and whispered, "Muy bonita, si, muy bonita." Lorenzo Pena then picked his six-foot-five-inch frame up from the table and disappeared through the closest exit, followed by his two bodyguards.

Chapter 6

Suddenly, Hardy was shaken from his daydream by the rumbling of the thick steel gate that obstructed the entrance to his cramped cell. The other men that shared the tiny enclosure with Hardy were returning from lunch in the mess hall. Johnny decided to spend the rest of the afternoon in the day room, so he swung down off his bunk and slipped on his red issued coveralls and loose open-back sandals. Stopping just a moment to think before he left the cell, he turned back to his bunk, reached up under his pillow and grabbed a pack of Winston cigarettes he had placed there earlier. Then sluggishly, he shuffled through the open doorway and down the narrow corridor that led to the large square area at the front of the cellblock.

The day room was a thirty-by-forty open area at the front of the cellblock, consisting of several metal tables and benches securely fastened to the concrete floor. At one end of the room, on each side, was a small shower stall and toilet. A dirty tattered shower curtain on the day room side, provided privacy from other inmates, while the side adjacent to the common corridor which led to the individual cells, was lined with thick steel bars, allowing the guards, male or female, to view the inmate while bathing. At the other end of the room, suspended from heavy metal cables, was a twenty-five-inch color TV that most inmates gathered around during sporting events and specials. Tucked away in the corner of the day room behind the television was a black rotary phone where local and collect calls could be made by anyone in the cellblock.

Johnny headed straight for the phone and dialed Nora's number. The phone rang at least a dozen times before she answered.

"Hello."

"Where the hell have you been? It's damn near 1:30."

"I was just out at my sister's making sure that we could use the van when...uh, I mean I could use the van again this week."

"Damn it!" he whispered softly into the phone. Just as he was about to explode, he paused to regain his composure and placed his hand over the receiver. He thought to himself, *Now is not the time to fly off the handle and screw everything up. Think. Relax and think!* There was a deafening silence on the phone for the next thirty seconds. To Nora it seemed as though an eternity had passed, but to Johnny, time didn't exist. His brain went into overdrive as various scenarios played out in front of him. He knew that the jail would never openly admit the fact that they monitored inmates' personal phone calls and violated their right to privacy. But, it was well-known among the inmates as well as other jail personnel that an informal policy had been established by the jail director himself authorizing his staff to randomly monitor inmate calls at the supervisor's discretion. Johnny had worked extremely hard at disarming the suspicions of the jail staff. At first, considering his past performances in this and many other jails, the staff had been on alert and deliberate with the safety precautions afforded a person with his reputation. But over the last eighteen months, he gradually disarmed both the staff and the administration by his commendable behavior whenever possible. This, coupled with the increasingly violent jail population and the shortage of staff members, had lowered his security risk status to the lowest level. To allow all his hard work and planning to go down the drain because this stupid little bitch made a slip of the tongue was just his luck.

What Hardy did not and could not know was that his luck was still with him. At the time of his phone call to Nora the two offices assigned to monitor the calls that day were distracted from their duty by a melee that had broken out in the booking area just moments before his call. All that was said was lost in the clamor of men running, voices yelling and chairs being thrown.

Attempting to change the subject and get right to his message he said, "Some joker just stepped all over my letter I had written to you. We just had a few words, everything's fine." He prayed that it was. "I'm gonna mail this letter to you tomorrow afternoon. They should pick it up in the day room about one o'clock, so it'll get to you by the weekend." Relieved that he had at least gotten her the information, he talked with her about irrelevant information for a few more minutes and then hung up.

Nora slowly placed the phone back on the receiver and sat down. What had she almost done? One tiny slip of the tongue and all the waiting, hoping and planning to be with the man she loved could all be wasted. Her body shivered, her head ached and she became nauseated. "Pull yourself together," she urged herself. She lay back on the sofa, elevated her feet on the arm and closed her eyes. What was it that he had said? She strained her brain till it hurt.

"I'm gonna mail this letter tomorrow afternoon...they'll pick it up about one o'clock."

That was it! Her headache was instantly replaced with panic as she swung her feet back onto the floor and forced herself to stand. Her legs were still a little weak and shaky, but they carried her to the kitchen. She had known this day would be coming, but she didn't know if she was ready yet! She retrieved her purse from the table where she threw it when she quickly entered the apartment to get the phone. Opening the purse she removed several pieces of paper—the list and two phone numbers. She grabbed the phone and dialed frantically.

The first call went to a residence in the Ballard area of north Seattle. The man she spoke with was neither surprised nor impressed. She merely told him who she was calling for and asked him to meet her the next day in Seattle at noon. No reasons were given, nor were any fees discussed. He simply asked what she would be driving, thanked her and hung up. Her next call was to the airline to confirm the two one-way airfares that she had purchased. Once the reservations were confirmed, she called Pena.

Lorenzo Pena was seated comfortably behind a narrow laminated conference table located in a small storefront he rented on Capitol Hill. He had just completed a business deal with two other "associates" when the phone rang. Pena raised his hand to silence the two as he answered the phone.

"Si"

"Is this Lorenzo Pena?"

"Si. Yo soy Lorenzo." Then sensing a need to speak English he repeated, "Yes, this is Lorenzo. Who is this?"

"This is Nora."

"Ah, Senorita. What a pleasure to speak with you again. And so soon. What can Lorenzo do for you?" Then he said almost as a tease, "Your wish, my beautiful one, is my command."

The charm in that smooth Latin voice removed any doubts she might have had and placed her in an unexpected dilemma. Under normal circumstances she would allow herself to be manipulated and seduced by such a handsome man. But these were not normal circumstances, and although she needed a man, this was not the time. She refocused her attention toward Johnny, removing the idea of her and Pena from her mind altogether.

"I must have the things we spoke of the other day. I need them tomorrow before noon." Authority seemed to return to her voice. "Can you deliver?"

His voice flowed like honey over the phone. "Why most certainly you can have them, Senorita. And at whatever time and place you desire."

What a smooth one, she thought. *It certainly would have been fun.* "I must have everything tomorrow at 11:30. You can deliver it to a parking stall on the south side of the Garfield play area on 23rd Avenue and East Alder. Do you know where that is?"

Half-laughing he replied, "Do I know where it is? Yes, pretty one, it is in my own back yard. It will be there as you ask. Have a pleasant day, Senorita, and give my warmest regards to our mutual friend." He hung up.

By the time she hung up the phone, the strength in her legs had returned. Her nausea continued but she decided it was due more to her sexual fantasy than anything else. For the remainder of the day, she studied maps of downtown Seattle and engraved in her head the route they would take, as well as one alternate route if things didn't go as planned. Either way, by tomorrow night her and his fate would be sealed.

Chapter 7

That evening Hardy ate dinner in the mess hall and then returned quickly to his cell to try and get as much rest as possible before the next afternoon. He tried relaxing on his bunk, on what he hoped would be his last night in captivity. But his affliction, common to one out of every ten people in the United States, refused him any comfort. He made no complaint though. If it weren't for a severe case of gastro-esophageal reflux, GERD (heartburn), the opportunity he had tomorrow would not have presented itself. The main symptoms are persistent heartburn and acid regurgitation. Some people, like Johnny, have GERD without heartburn. Instead, they experience pain in the chest, hoarseness in the morning, or trouble swallowing. You may feel like you have food stuck in your throat or like you are choking or your throat is tight. These symptoms can sometimes be mistaken for a heart attack.

Under normal circumstances in the state reformatory, medical tests and treatment for this ailment could be done safely inside the facility. But since Hardy's appeals were being dragged through the system and his sentence to the state reformatory virtually put on hold, the state was reluctant to house him within their own overcrowded facility until there was a more definite decision on his future. Therefore, the King County facility was forced to treat his medical condition. Since the facility did not have the equipment or the staff to perform the type of medical tests he needed, he was sent outside the facility to the County Hospital, located about a quarter of a mile directly east of the jail where several of the city's largest hospitals are located on what is commonly referred to as "Pill Hill."

He recalled the first time this ailment struck him almost two years ago. He was living in the Portland area and overindulging in everything from cigarettes and drugs to alcohol and greasy fast food. He had noticed one night in bed a sharp pain in his upper chest area followed by a tightening of his throat. So severe was the pain that followed, that within twenty minutes an aid car from the local fire department was summoned and he was on his way to the emergency room. He thought for sure that he was having a heart attack. He wound up at the hospital for two days with doctors and nurses prodding and poking him for the better part of the time. When released he was placed on a bland diet and ordered to eliminate coffee and cigarettes. The doctors had told him that if he continued to abuse himself as he was doing, he had an 80% chance of developing a hernia and was at risk of developing Barrett's esophagus. This precancerous condition is characterized by chronic acid reflux, in which acids and other digestive juices escape from the stomach, flow backward into the esophagus, and may cause heartburn, which increases the risk of cancer of the esophagus.

When he recovered from this bout, he realized how he might use this malady and its symptoms to his advantage if he were ever caught and placed in jail again. He explained the plan to Nora, who, having heard the diagnosis of the doctors, was not overly enthusiastic about the possibility of his scheme backfiring on him and causing him permanent damage or even death. But she finally agreed to its plausibility and decided that she would help if that situation arose.

Since he was arrested, Hardy had systematically increased

his consumption of coffee, cigarettes, marijuana smuggled in through a cooperative social worker, and spicy food, whenever it was available. Now his condition worsened daily. At first, he was treated in the jail infirmary where he was escorted to and from by a member of the jail staff. Recently his condition had worsened to the point that the jail staff and doctors decided that it was necessary to have a full battery of tests done at the County Hospital. This decision was spurred on by a severe attack he had just two weeks before. The medic unit was called and he was taken to the emergency room at the County Hospital. He was treated that evening and released back to the jail after he was provided some relief through medication they gave him. It was then that the doctors told him further tests were necessary and an appointment would be scheduled through the jail infirmary.

When he returned to the jail the next morning, he sent word through the grapevine to a friend who worked in the infirmary. He needed to know when that appointment would be set. That same day he received word that the appointment would be made the following week, and he would get the day and time as soon as it was scheduled.

As he lay in his bunk, he smiled slightly to himself. He needed only to put up with this for a short time more. By this time tomorrow, he'd be far away.

Chapter 8

At seven o'clock the portable Big Ben alarm clock woke Nora from a fitful night's sleep. She reached out from under the covers, turned off the clock and rolled over. Suddenly realizing what day it was, she threw off the covers, leapt naked from the sofa bed and dashed into the kitchen where she started the coffee maker. From the kitchen she went directly into the bathroom, turned on the shower and got in. As she emerged from the shower, the cool air along with a sense of anticipation caused her skin to tingle and the nipples on her breasts to harden. She hurriedly toweled off and dressed in tight jeans, a short-sleeve white silk blouse and white tennis shoes (all new rewards from her latest excursion). She placed her hair in a tight bun on the top of her head with two large combs and then neatly applied makeup to her eyes. When she was done, she returned to the kitchen and poured herself a cup of strong black coffee. While she drank, she mentally went over a checklist of things to do that morning.

First on her list was to pack a bag, which she did after her first cup of coffee. In her bag she packed all the items she felt were essential to her own survival for the next couple of months. She also packed a bag for Johnny. Anything else they needed would have to be purchased later on after their arrival. Next she phoned her sister and told her where she could pick up her van that afternoon. She purposely refused to tell her sister, who she had secretly let in on their plans, where they would be going. Although she trusted her entirely, she knew Johnny would blow a fuse if he even found out her sister knew that much. Besides, if her sister didn't know where they were, she couldn't possible tell anyone, especially the police, even if she wanted to. When she hung up the phone, she set out around the apartment to find anything that might tie her or Johnny to the apartment. Bills, letters and pictures were all gathered together and placed on the kitchen table. Then one by one she went through all of them. Those she could pack she did. Those not important enough to pack she placed in a paper sack which she immediately brought to the garbage dumpster. When she was sure she had disposed of everything, she relaxed and lit a cigarette. In the last month or so, she'd developed into quite a chain smoker. Between cigarettes and her addiction, she barely was able to keep up with everyday living expenses. Now, at least for a short time, they would live comfortably on the money Johnny had stashed away...and what she could refund this morning. It was a chance she had to take but she dared not tell Johnny. He would be furious that she would even think of risking everything for just a few dollars. But strangely, she felt that she had to contribute to their partnership. She wanted to feel worthy of his love and she would do anything to prove it. Quickly she took one last look at the apartment. In her entire adult life she could not remember living in any one place longer. With a sense of loss in her heart and tears in her eyes, she locked the door behind her and headed out to the van.

Placing the key in the ignition, she looked in the rear view mirror and peered at bag after bag of new clothing still tagged and in their original packaging lying in the rear of the van. She and her sister had worked for hours yesterday at Bellevue Square, a huge upscale suburban mall on the eastside of Lake

Washington. Once during the day they thought they had been spotted by a pair of store security officers, later only to find out that they were being hounded by a couple of horny bachelors looking for an easy lay. By the time they shook the two hounds, who followed them into McDonald's on the main level of the two-story mall and tried to pick them up, they had accumulated a small fortune of expensive clothing, shoes and jewelry.

Nora checked her watch as she started the van. It was 8:30. She had three and a half-hours before she had to be downtown Seattle. She had chosen to return most of the items to another mall, south of Seattle, just outside the city of Tukwila, because of its close proximity and easy access to both Interstates 5 and 405 and the fact that most of the stores at the mall would refund her cash without a receipt. For that reason, plus the fact that it was very unlikely anyone at the mall stores would recognize her from her foray the day before, reducing the chances of a mishap or an arrest, she chose the South Center Mall for her last big payday.

Chapter 9

At 7:30 in the morning the steel barred door rolled back and Hardy shuffled down to the day room. His night had been uncomfortable at best. Every time he tried to recline in his bunk, the acid would rush back through the muscles of his stomach into his esophagus causing extreme pain in his chest. He knew it was the gallons of coffee and dozens of cigarettes he had indulged in recently, but after today that would not matter. When he and Nora got to where they were going, he had a friend that would set him up in a private clinic where his corroded insides could be treated and his identity would not be questioned. For the time being, he was prepared for the day's exciting activities.

He showered in the day room, combed his shoulder length hair and untangled his scraggly beard. He had purposely allowed both to grow much longer than he ever had in the past. In fact, the addition of so much hair prompted the jail staff to update his mug shot on file for better identification purposes. Exactly what he had hoped for. Why was it that the authorities were always so predictable? What fools! So far they had played right into his hand. After he cleaned up he put on new jail coveralls provided to him by the guards. This was standard procedure whenever an inmate was transported outside the facility, as he would be this afternoon. The bright iridescent color used on transported inmates would make him easily identifiable in the County Hospital where many employees were clad in different colored jump suits. Once he changed, he took a seat at one of the day room tables, picked up a deck of cards and awaited the passing of the morning.

Chapter 10

A tan sedan sat parked along the roadway just south of the Seattle Ferry Terminal at Pier 52. Inside the sedan sat a short, squat man with a crew cut. The hard line of his jaw and his deep-set eyes were what Nora noticed immediately. She was sure this was the man she was supposed to meet. It was already a quarter to twelve and she was running dangerously late. Everything depended on timing. She had not expected it to take so long at the South Center Mall, but the reward for her patience was great. In her purse, along with the money she had taken from the safety deposit box, was now another envelope containing over five thousand dollars in cash. She was sure that if they returned to Seattle at a later date, she would need an entire new set of ID. The three aliases she used today would surely be on every major store's "hot list" by next week.

She pulled the van against the curb across the street from the sedan. The man, in his late fifties, looked over and gently nodded his head in her direction. After she acknowledged the nod, the man got out of his car and walked across the street toward the van. He had massive wide shoulders and a relatively slender waist for a man his age. As he approached the car, she spotted a distinctive limp. She recalled a conversation she had with Johnny several years before. She asked him if he was ever afraid of anyone. He was just about to put on that macho act when he stopped himself and said that there was one man. His name was Hank Kruger. Real short, solidly built guy with a Dick Butkus hairdo. He had a slight limp from a bullet he took during an armored car robbery years ago. Kruger was a guy that even Johnny respected, one you would sure hate to have as an enemy. On the other hand, he's just the kind of guy you want in a jam.

The stocky man with the limp walked around to the passenger side of the car, opened the door and slid into the van, his bulky frame completely filling the passenger seat.

"Hi, I'm Hank."

Chapter 11

Franklin J. Pierce had been a corrections officer for almost seven years. At thirty-seven he had been divorced for three years and was a proud father to twin boys. In February of last year, he was transferred from third-shift at the jail as a deck officer to day-shift as a transporting officer on the court detail. As in every other section of the jail, the shortage of manpower mandated that as part of every working day, he be assigned to the secondary task of transporting prisoners back and forth from the jail to the County Hospital.

When he came to work that day, he was feeling a little under the weather. He was out late the night before at a new girlfriend's house on Queen Ann Hill, where, to his disappointment, he hadn't even gotten close to scoring. And to add insult to injury, he got drunk in his attempt to impress this woman and made a complete ass out of himself. Feeling depressed because of his performance the night before, Pierce was not overly excited about being assigned to the infirmary when he first started his shift.

"Shit, they could at least let me wake up before they stick me with this crap," were his first words of the morning.

The first run of the day was an inmate who had been beaten in the day room of one of the cellblocks earlier that morning. The poor bastard had been beaten to a pulp, and probably had multiple fractures, as well as abrasions, cuts and a concussion. The aid crew loaded him into the ambulance and delivered both he and the inmate to the emergency room at Harborview Hospital within a few minutes. There he waited with the inmate until the doctor finished his examination and bandaged him up. By that time, it was 10:30 and his shift was already almost half over. At 10:45 a.m., a white jail van with a county jail insignia painted in dull brown on both front doors, drove up to the emergency room exit to pick them up. He escorted the prisoner into the rear of the county van, strapped him into his seat with the seat belt then sat down across from him as the van took its short trip down the hill back to the jail. When he returned, he got the news from his boss that he was assigned to another hospital trip at one o'clock that afternoon. It would probably run into some overtime, but it had already been approved.

"Just what I need," he grumbled as he walked down the corridor to the officers' dining area. The small, dimly lit little room, just off the jail kitchen, normally held five to eight officers at any given time of the day. Today no one other than Pierce was there. There were some bologna and cheese sandwiches out on the counter. He picked one up, looked disdainfully at the dried meat between the two pieces of bread and threw it back down on the counter. He walked over, poured himself a cup of hot coffee and grabbed two sugar cookies from a plate next to the coffeepot.

"At least there's something good to eat around here," he mumbled as he took a seat at the table. He was ready for anything…except another trip back to the hospital.

At twelve o'clock he returned to the infirmary and prepared the paperwork necessary to take his next inmate to the hospital. While he filled out the name of the inmate on the appropriate forms he had gathered at the infirmary desk, the nurse asked if he would prefer the aid unit again. Pierce checked the security risk list posted in the infirmary then turned toward the nurse.

"Nah, piece of cake. I'll take this one myself."

Just then Johnny Hardy walked into the infirmary and signed in.

Chapter 12

While the van traveled eastbound on Yesler Way toward the Garfield play area, Nora explained to Kruger exactly what was going down.

"It's a pretty risky situation, don't you think?" Kruger said with a grimace.

Hearing the uneasiness in his voice she verbally stroked him. "It's got its problems, but Johnny said if anyone could help pull it off, it would be you."

"Well, of course I can pull this thing off," he said almost offended. "But what I'm worried about is that spic friend of yours. Is this guy just another spic full of bullshit or can he really put his money where his big spic mouth is?"

It was obvious from the start that Kruger was not impressed with anyone with a Spanish surname. Thank God neither one would have to meet.

Before she realized what she was saying, the words blurted from her mouth, "Don't worry about Pena. He'll take care of his end of the bargain; you just worry about taking care of your end." She glanced over at Kruger and a moment of panic came over her. His deep-set eyes were literally bulging from their sockets as he stared across the van at her. Just when she thought she had blown it, the ends of his mouth turned up into a big grin and he began to laugh.

"You know, lady, you got balls. I mean not real ones," he fumbled, "but balls just the same. I like you. I should have figured what kind of dame you were when you told me who your boyfriend was." Finally, with the ice broken between them, the van sped up Capitol Hill toward their first destination.

On 23rd Avenue, she turned left three blocks south of the park, and slowed down to twenty miles per hour. Their heads scanned the surrounding blocks for any sign of the police. As they reached East Alder and 23rd, she spotted what she was looking for. There, off to her right, parked just south of the play field as Pena said it would be, was a long white linen truck used to make pickups and deliveries of soiled and clean products from businesses in the area.

Nora parked their van on the east side of 25th and Jefferson. Before they got out, she reached into her purse and grabbed a plain white envelope. She handed the envelope to Kruger who, without ever opening it, folded it neatly and placed it in his pants pocket. That being done, they both got out of the van and cautiously approached the linen truck. When they were certain there was no one around, they got in, Kruger driving and Nora on the passenger side. She climbed her way over the dirty linen on the floor between them and into the back of the truck. There on a shelf she found everything she had asked for. A set of handcuff keys, a bolt cutter, a sawed-off shotgun with a dozen rounds of ammo, a semiautomatic handgun, a stainless steel Ruger Security Six .357 magnum, a map, three white uniforms for them to slip into and two black ski masks for her and Kruger.

"I guess your spic friend can produce after all."

"Yes, he certainly can." She smiled as she looked at the note left on the shelf. It read, "To a beautiful woman, may I see more of you, much more, the next time we meet." Behind the note she found a bottle of twelve-year-old scotch. She doubted very much that she and Johnny would have time to share it that afternoon.

Chapter 13

Hardy took a seat in the infirmary while Pierce finished filling out the paperwork. At 12:30, Pierce got up from the desk. With little enthusiasm he said, "Let's get going, Hardy."

Without a word, Hardy was up from of his chair and headed out the infirmary door ahead of Pierce. He had walked about ten paces when the effects of the attack from the night before caught up with him. He slowed down, hunched over and began to shuffle down the hallway.

"You're looking pretty ragged today," Pierce said with some pity in his voice.

"Yeah, tough night last night. Didn't sleep much."

"Well I guess every night's a tough night in here, isn't it?"

Pierce's question went unanswered and the two men continued down the hallway toward the electronic gate. The gate clicked open as Hardy pushed it back and entered the booking area. He sat in the same familiar holding cell in the corner of the room while Pierce retrieved his gun belt, car keys and a waist belt and cuffs for him. As he sat in the cell watching the intake officers process new arrivals at the jail, he couldn't help but glance at the clock behind the booking counter. It was 12:40. His anxiety began to heighten and he became fidgety.

Pierce returned and opened the cell not a moment too soon. Hardy quickly stepped out of the cell and as he had become accustomed, place his hands on a nearby wall, stepped back and spread his legs. Pierce, impressed with Hardy's cooperation, made a crucial error. He, as so many other good men do, mentally dropped his guard and allowed himself to believe that this was just another normal run-of-the-mill hospital transport. His prisoner was sick; he needn't fear anything from him. He would merely transport him to the hospital, read the papers while the doctors treated him and then return him to the jail where he would then pack up and go home knowing his next paycheck would reflect the extra time worked. After a quick pat-down he placed the chain belt around Hardy's waist. Attached to the front of the chain were a set of handcuffs, which Hardy readily slipped into. The two men passed through the electronically controlled door and out into the small foyer in front of the elevator. Pierce pushed the elevator button and then went over to the gun locker to retrieve his gun. When the elevator arrived both men stepped in and they were transported to the parking level where their jail vehicle was waiting.

Chapter 14

The white linen truck sat alone on the corner of 8th Avenue and James Street. Kruger checked his watch as he sat in his white uniform behind the wheel of the truck. It was 12:45. Nora sat on a pile of dirty laundry in the back of the truck nervously fingering the ski mask she would soon don.

"You sure this is the route they'll take?" Kruger asked for the fourth or fifth time.

Engrossed in her own thoughts and worries, she looked up, puzzled, not understanding what he had said.

"The route! The route!" he shouted nervously. "Are you sure this is the right one?"

Finally returning to reality she blurted, "Yes, yes, I'm sure!" Just then she looked up through the front windshield and saw the county car. "There he is!" she yelled.

A white Dodge Diplomat equipped with a silent partner, a metal screen between the front and back seats to protect the driver from the occupants in the rear, turned southbound from James onto 8th Avenue toward the hospital one block away. In the rear seat she could see Johnny. The light for southbound traffic turned green and the laundry truck proceeded through the intersection. When the truck reached the hospital, the Dodge had already pulled up to the designated jail parking area outside the emergency room. While the truck pulled up into the "no parking" zone behind the jail car, Pierce opened his driver's door, reached back and manually released the rear door lock located inside the doorframe on the driver's side. It was then that Pierce made his second mistake as he got out of the car. Like so many officers who get into the habit of doing things routinely, he simply neglected to do a very simple thing. He never bothered to look at his surroundings. Instead, he chose to accept them for what he believed they were from the numerous trips he had made before. Had he taken just a moment to look before he opened Johnny's door, he would have noticed the white linen truck pulling up behind him in a "no parking anytime" zone. He might also have seen the two individuals emerging from that truck in ski masks, armed with weapons. Before Pierce realized what was happening, the butt of a .12-gauge shotgun came crashing down, splitting the back of his head wide open and driving him face-first into the pavement where he momentarily lost consciousness.

Johnny sprang like a cat from the back seat of the car onto the pavement above Pierce. Nora met him there, still in her ski mask, gun tucked into the waistband of her white uniform. She quickly snipped the waist chain from his body with the pair of bolt cutters taken from the truck. Then Johnny and Nora headed for the truck with Kruger limping close behind. Suddenly, two shots rang out. Pierce, who had regained consciousness on the pavement, had enough presence of mind to wait until all three had started back toward the truck before he dragged himself up onto the rear quarter panel of his car. He pulled out his revolver and shot Hank Kruger dead. Instinctively, at the sound of the shots, Johnny grabbed the Ruger from Nora's waistband, spun around and with his hands still in handcuffs fired a quick burst of three rounds, dispatching Franklin J. Pierce.

He pushed Nora through the passenger door of the truck and into the driver's seat. Nora, still stunned from the scene she had just witnessed, obeyed without a word.

"You drive," he yelled, "NOW!"

As the truck pulled away from the curb, all hell broke loose outside the doorway of the emergency room. Emergency medical personnel scrambled out the exit toward the two men in the street. Others, who had witnessed the incident, were now descending upon the street from shelter they had taken during the gunfight. In all the confusion, everyone had forgotten to do one very crucial thing—call the police. It was at least five minutes before the first emergency call came into 911 operators in Seattle, giving Johnny his biggest break of the day. No one really knew whether or not the five minutes would have made the difference in his or her capture. But two officers working that section of the hill that afternoon, swore they saw the white linen truck drive by them as they drove past the Garfield play area just three minutes before receiving the "shots fired" call.

Chapter 15

The truck sped off eastbound from the hospital to Boren Avenue where Nora made a right turn. Two blocks later she turned left on East Alder and headed directly toward the Garfield play area. Now over her initial shock, she was riding the high of an adrenaline surge. She had driven this route a dozen times or more in the last week and at least several hundred times in her head. As the truck crossed over 23rd Avenue, Johnny had already freed himself from the handcuffs and removed his jail-issued overalls. She spotted the getaway van and pulled the truck up ahead of it. It had been parked there earlier that day by one of Pena's men just as he said it would be. Quickly she removed her white uniform, revealing her jeans and silk blouse below. Rolling the ski mask and the uniform up in a ball, she stuffed it under the front seat. Johnny, removed a dirty pair of work overalls from one of the laundry baskets, placed them on, opened the rear door of the truck and with the automatic tucked snugly in his pants, stepped out and took his first breath of free air in almost a year and a half. "Wonderful," he said to himself, and vowed then and there that he would never be captured again.

Nora jumped out of the truck into his arms. He felt her two breasts against his chest and as the scent of her perfume filled his nostrils, he had to muster all his strength to push her away.

"Not now, but soon." Then he hurried to the sliding door of the van and got in. Nora closed the back door of the linen truck and hurried to the front of the van. As she got in she froze. She spotted a police car cruising up 25th in her side view mirror.

"The cops!" she blurted out to Johnny as he pulled on a Grateful Dead T-shirt she had gotten him.

"Have they seen us?" He reached for the gun in his waistband.

"I don't think so. They're about a block away."

"Just start the car, and would you fuckin' just look like you belong here!" Johnny lay on the floor behind the driver's seat with the automatic gripped tightly in his hand. The silence was deafening and the few seconds it took for the patrol car to pass were like minutes.

"They're gone."

"Good, now let's get the hell out of here."

"What about Hank?"

"Hank's dead. He's not our problem now."

The van pulled out and made its way northbound to Cherry Street, where it turned west toward Interstate 5. At the top of the hill as she crossed over Broadway, Cherry turned into James Street. It was there that she actually realized their escape route took them within one block of the hospital. Just brazen enough to get away with it. As she passed the hospital she expected to see police in the area, but not as many as she now saw. By the time she reached 8th and James, traffic was snarled and it seemed as though every other car was a police car. She waited patiently for her turn to pass through the cluttered intersection as Johnny lay quietly on the floor. Finally she got through the congestion and without further delay she took the southbound ramp to Interstate 5.

As the van made its way southbound along the freeway toward Sea-Tac Airport, Johnny sat up and pulled the black velvet curtain hanging behind the driver's seat across the width of the van, blocking her view of him. Now, more than ever, if he were to make his escape good, he had to use every skill he had acquired over the years. Right now, the problem was how to get on the plane without being identified. The jail had unwittingly helped him a great deal. By the time he boarded the flight this afternoon, he imagined every law enforcement officer in western Washington would be looking for him. But who would they really be looking for? Thanks to the updated jail mug shot they would probably be looking for that long-haired bushy bearded guy who left the jail this afternoon. The snip of scissors and hum of the electric razor droned on behind the curtain as he set to work with the items she had brought along.

Nora was careful to stay within the speed limit and after about fifteen minutes the van exited Interstate 5 onto Highway 518, which led directly to the airport exit. Driving past the time and temperature sign located at the entrance of the airport Nora followed the signs to the parking garage adjacent to the main terminal and drove in. She wound up the spiral cement ramps to the third floor (just as good a floor as any to get lost on), pulled into a parking space among hundreds of other cars and turned off the motor. Johnny pushed aside the curtain and she could hardly believe her eyes. Gone was the unkempt sandy brown hair that once grew in abundance. Gone was the bushy beard that had covered most of his face. In its place was a smooth baby-like face and short military haircut. In addition he had changed the color of his eyes with the contact lens she brought for him, and had added a small two-inch scar that went horizontally across his forehead just below the hairline.

"How do I look?"

"My God, I can't believe you sometimes." She reached out and pulled him close to her for the first time in many months, and their emotions ignited. His hands immediately found their way to her firm breasts where he gently pinched her swollen nipples. She pulled his mouth hungrily to hers and ravaged his waiting lips. As they began to lose themselves to their desires, the reality of the situation suddenly flashed through his mind. He must control his urge just a little while longer.

Against her determined strength to merge there and then, he pushed their bodies apart. She pled softly as she lay on the floor where their lust had taken them. But he was more determined now than ever not to do something that might cause him his freedom. There would be plenty of time for this and more once they were out of the area.

He got to his knees and tucked in his shirt. Seeing the situation was futile, she got off the floor of the van and began to button her blouse. He slid open the van's door and stepped out. Reaching in for the two suitcases that she had packed, he patted her on the butt. She turned eagerly, only to find him holding the suitcases and waiting for her. She hopped from the van and joined him. They walked to the parking garage elevator and headed for the main terminal. Once in the terminal, among the thousands of other travelers they became just two additional faces in the crowd.

As they walked through the terminal toward the boarding gate, he was disturbed when he noticed the unusually long line waiting to pass through the entry checkpoint. When they reached the line, he saw the reason for the delay. Nora grabbed his hand and froze. There at the front of the line stood two Port of Seattle police officers. One of the officers held a faxed photo in his hand. One by one the passengers passed the officer's inspection and walked through the check point. Then it was their turn. To his surprise, and to her relief, the officers, without as much as a second glance, waved them through with a smile. His hunch had been right after all. Hundreds of servicemen passed through the airport every day. No one would be expecting him to look like this. They walked through the checkpoint and onto the boarding area. With smiles on their faces, they disappeared down the ramp and onto their plane.

As they took their seats on the Boeing 727, a strange feeling came over him. It was not like him to be forgetful, but had the heightened intensity of the day's activities caused him to overlook something? Whatever it was it was eating at his insides. That's when he noticed his chest tightening. Taking several deep breaths and sitting back in his seat, he tried to rid himself of this ominous feeling. As the plane taxied to the runway, it was as if a bolt of lightning struck him. On the way to the airport, in his haste to change, he had hidden the Ruger used to gun down the correction officer under the small refrigerator in the back of the van. In the heat of the moment before they got out, coupled with their rush to get to the gate, he had forgotten to take it and dispose of it the way he had planned. A dark mood descended over him and for the remainder of the flight he remained silent.

Chapter 16

It was nearly six o'clock in the evening. Neither he nor his partner had a day off in over two weeks. They would continue to work double shifts until the uneasiness in the community subsided and they finally had this low-life scum bucket off the street.

But then, this was the life he had chosen for himself. A life filled daily with contradictions of his own beliefs. He often said if he had it all to do over again knowing what he knew now, he would probably be a garbage man. After all, wasn't that what a cop really was: a human garbage man. But he knew, deep down inside, that he could never be anything else but a cop. Being a cop was a job that consumed your body and soul, seven days a week, fifty-two weeks a year for twenty years…or more.

At six feet tall, 195 pounds, with an olive complexion and jet black hair, this second-generation cop had worked his way up from street cop to plainclothes detective, paying his dues as a beat cop and never forgetting his roots on the street. His career as a street cop and detective spanned nearly two decades. Although lately he had been heard saying this was a young man's job and he didn't want to be rolling around on the ground with these young punks when he reached fifty, the truth was, the passion he had for his work had not decrease as his years increased, as it all too often happened to men in his position. Instead of looking for a nice cushy place within the department to settle back and retire, he somehow always found himself right smack in the middle of things. He always had the knack for police work and caught onto the tricks of the trade faster than most. Married to a far too understanding wife, with two young children, he often found it hard to communicate his deep feelings to the ones he loved the most. He never talked much at home about his work. It was his way of insulating his loved ones from the insanity that had become part of his daily life. His wife understood the man she married and never really questioned his love or loyalty to her or his work, but supported him and was always there when he needed her. And for this, he couldn't love and appreciate her enough.

As he sat on that same uncomfortable red vinyl bench seat he had sat on for the past two weeks for nearly twelve hours a day, Bob DeNucci began to feel a strange uneasiness come over him. He shifted slightly to the left in the booth where he sat, allowing the hard rubber grip on his 9mm Smith and Wesson semi-automatic to protrude ever so slightly from the shoulder holster on the left side of his navy blue goose down jacket. His partner, having just entered the *Guinness Book of World Records* for the most coffee consumed in one hour, got up from the table and gingerly strolled to the men's room at the rear of the small greasy spoon café. While he sat alone, his view through the plate glass window at the front of the tiny café was unobstructed. Across the parking lot of the strip mall where they waited he eyed the surroundings of the state-run liquor store with hawk-like vigilance, waiting and hoping for his prey to arrive. His partner, looking very much relieved, returned to the table and plopped down on the seat across from him.

"Ready for another cup?" Bob held his mug high in the air to attract the attention of the waitress.

"No, I'll pass this time. Anything new since I left?"

Andy Anderson was no stranger to long stakeouts. A veteran officer with half dozen years of experience in the ghettos of Los Angeles before moving to the Seattle area and joining the County Police Department, he had spent most of the last six months on special stakeouts such as this. Had the handsome, curly haired blond surfer been married, Bob was sure the pace of these last six months would have surely done him in.

While he waited for the waitress to get to the table, a thought crossed his mind and a smile came to his face. He thought back to the last time the two had spent this much time on a stakeout; a dry cleaners not more than a mile from where they now sat. They had spent two weeks sitting behind the front counter of the cleaners staking out an all-night doughnut shop across the parking lot, waiting for the same dirt bag to hit the shop for the third time. Of course, he never did show up. But that didn't prevent them from having a little excitement. When was it? The second week they were there, both sitting behind the counter on empty five-gallon cans of cleaner fluid they had taken from the back of the store. There in the dark drinking coffee and chuckling about some of the calls they had responded to lately. Andy leaned back a little too far and had fallen off his makeshift chair. In a futile attempt to prevent his full cup of coffee from spraying halfway across the cleaners, Andy reached back to grab the flying projectile when he accidentally tripped the audible burglary alarm. Instantly, the lights in the cleaners came on and blinked continuously. The alarm bell blared and a horn shrieked through the silent night alerting everything that lived and breathed within a five-square block area of their presence. As Andy continued his fall to the floor, he was greeted by a bundle of dirty laundry that had fallen off a shelf he bumped on the way down. The clothing, soaked in black coffee, literally covered Andy from head to foot as he lay on the floor helplessly laughing. Bob did not escape the calamity of the moment either. And as Andy hit the floor his right leg struck the empty bucket that Bob had been sitting on, sending it and Bob sprawling across the floor of the cleaners. As he lay there on the floor, his hot ceramic mug of coffee catapulted over the front counter where it shattered inches from the plate glass window at the front of the store. It took them twenty minutes to disarm the alarm, all the time laughing as tears fell from their eyes. Once the alarm had been disarmed, they pretty much figured that their presence had been compromised and decided to call off that stage of the stakeout.

Of course, at the time, they could not have known the suspect had been just blocks away preparing for another assault on the doughnut shop when the alarm went off. He witnessed the spectacle, put two and two together and decided to put off his hit that morning. About a week later, the first of the liquor store robberies occurred. Within a week, there were over a dozen. When the crime analysis office put all the information together at the precinct, both Bob and Andy knew it was their guy and the stakeouts began again.

The waitress finished pouring Bob his coffee, then with a smile placed a small piece of paper, upside down, next to Anderson's empty coffee cup before departing for the kitchen.

"Not again!" Bob protested, as Andy placed the tiny scrap of paper in his wallet. "This is the third waitress in this place to pass you her number. When the hell do you get time to take care of that stable of yours?"

"Elementary, my dear Watson. I..."

But before he could continue, something caught Bob's attention. His eye was drawn to a movement in the alley across the parking lot, some fifty feet east of the front doors of the liquor store. At first glance it seemed nothing more than the movement of an animal, a cat or dog perhaps. But to the trained and experienced eye, something was askew.

Suddenly, a tall, slender figure dressed in khaki pants, green fatigue jacket and yellow construction helmet shot out from the darkness of the alley. As he made the turn from the alley onto the sidewalk at a fast gallop, there was no doubt in either cop's mind what was going down. Both men quickly slid from their seats in the café and headed for the front door. As Andy alerted other officers in the area with his portable, Bob couldn't help but feel there was something peculiar about this figure, in profile, that he had missed; something that had not been present in the surveillance pictures taken at the other liquor stores that were robbed. As they went out the door the notion slipped into the back of his mind and vanished in the next few minutes of confusion.

Andy followed Bob across the lot to a prearranged location where their vehicles, each containing a .12-gauge shotgun with pistol grips for easy deployment, were strategically parked, cutting off the east and west escape routes from the liquor store. Six days prior the suspect had robbed another liquor store at N. 155th Street and Aurora Avenue N. In all the excitement of the robbery, the two officers on that stakeout had forgotten that there was a back door to the liquor store and the suspect had escaped. On the off-chance the suspect decided to exit the rear, the first patrol unit to the scene, now about three blocks away, was directed to respond to the back of the building. As Bob took up his position east of the liquor store, careful not to expose his back to the alley where an accomplice might be looking on, the suspect, already in the store, bounded across the front counter with a gun he had just taken from under his coat; if the surveillance photos held true, it was a sawed-off shotgun. Next he herded the dazed employees, together with two customers, into the back room. The two males and three females were ordered to strip off their clothing and place them in a pile in the center of the room. When he was sure everyone was more concerned about their appearance than his presence, he proceeded to empty the open safe of all of its cash. Then, as if forgotten at first, he returned to the till in the front of the store where he quickly removed all the bills and left the bulky change behind.

Murphy's Law *prov.* The correct, *original* Murphy's Law reads: "If there are two or more ways to do something, and one of those ways can result in a catastrophe, then someone will do it."

Edward A. Murphy, Jr. was one of the engineers on the rocket-sled experiments that were done by the U.S. Air Force in 1949 to test human acceleration tolerances (USAF project MX981). One experiment involved a set of sixteen accelerometers mounted to different parts of the subject's body. There were two ways each sensor could be glued to its mount, and somebody methodically installed all sixteen the wrong way around. Murphy then made the original form of his pronouncement, which the test subject (Major John Paul Stapp) quoted at a news conference a few days later.

Within months, Murphy's Law had spread to various technical cultures connected to aerospace engineering. Before too many years had gone by variants had passed into the popular imagination, changing as they went. Most of these are variants on "Anything that can go wrong will." This is correctly referred to as Finagle's Law. The mimetic drift apparent in these mutants clearly demonstrates Murphy's Law acting on itself! (*Jargon Dictionary, (www.netmeg.net*)

It was during this critical period of time, when the suspect was inside the store emptying the till, that Murphy's Law raised its ugly head. As Andy took up a position behind his car parked just west of the liquor store, he withdrew his shotgun from the rear floorboard on the driver's side. Moving up the vehicle to get better protection behind the engine block of the car, he noticed, to his disbelief, a group of six Girl Scouts and their shapely blond leader scamper from a silver Ford station wagon parked on the west side of the liquor store. The first two girls turned the corner of the building and were so intent on beginning their cookie sale that they ran right in front of Andy's car toward the front door of the liquor store.

Instantly, Anderson slid across the hood of his car landing feet first on the pavement, gun in hand, scaring the hell out of the poor young woman and the four remaining girls.

That's when Bob first saw the suspect headed toward the front door.

"He's comin', get the girls!" DeNucci yelled frantically.

Operating solely on instinct and adrenaline, Anderson propped his shotgun against the car and sprinted toward the doorway, where the two bewildered children, now scared and crying, stood frozen in the path of the suspect. With a swoop of his giant hands, Anderson scooped up the two girls, then turned and ran in an effort to reach the safety of his car before the suspect realized what was happening. Suddenly, the Girl Scout leader screamed. Bob, who up until that moment had all his attention focused on the suspect, momentarily glanced toward Andy and froze in horror. In his haste to get to safety with both girls, he had tripped and now lay face down upon the sidewalk. As the suspect exited the store, he seemed to sense the danger at hand. He stopped, and for a brief second reflected on the shotgun against the car and the blond man with two young girls beneath him sprawled on the concrete, not more than twenty feet in front of him.

At that very second, Bob began to feel a pit deep in the bottom of his stomach. His attention immediately reverted back to the figure looming over his partner. What he saw he wasn't quite prepared for. The uneasy feeling he had put behind him as the suspect first entered the store now came to life in the form of an ugly lifelike Halloween mask. As if he were a lifeless participant in B-grade horror flick, he stared as the grotesque creature stopped and took point-blank aim at his partner. His vision badly hampered by the mask, the suspect was unaware of DeNucci's presence. As he raised the sawed-off shotgun to waist height and began to apply pressure to the trigger, a deafening explosion ripped through the evening.

Chapter 17

The medical terminology for this phenomenon includes phrases like "trance behavior," "time distortion" and "instinctive survival response." What occurred next is found to be a normal reaction in many police officers involved in shooting situations. DeNucci never heard the blast of his .12-gauge as it lit up the night and deafened most of the witnesses at the scene. What he does recall was the split second decision he made to save his partner's life. After that, everything seemed to slow down to slow motion. What really took only a matter of seconds seemingly took minutes to play out in front of him.

As he pulled the trigger of his shotgun, he recalled seeing the pellets explode from the end of the thick black barrel and glide slowly through the air toward their final destination. The steel pellets smashed into the right side of the suspect's skull, just behind the bizarre mask with the sunken eyes, misshapen nose and large ugly warts, causing large chunks of scalp and skull to rip away from his head. The suspect was lifted off the sidewalk two feet into the air and thrown nose-first into the cement walkway five feet from where Anderson, visibly shaken, sat watching in disbelief.

Time returned to normal and Bob racked another round into the chamber of his shotgun as he slowly proceeded out from behind his car, careful not to allow any bystanders or witnesses in his line of fire. Meanwhile, Andy, bleeding from a cut on his forearm as well as one from his right knee where his new Levi's had ripped away, had managed to pull himself to his feet and was leaning unsteadily against the front fender of his car. As DeNucci approached the suspect, who by now was lying in a pool of crimson, he could hear the sirens of the approaching patrol cars. When he finally reached the suspect, a sawed-off shotgun and a canvas bag containing the money from the robbery were beside him. He gently nudged the gun away with his foot, careful not to disturb any other evidence. After a quick but thorough scan of the area for accomplices, he placed his shotgun down out of the reach of the suspect, drew his service revolver from the leather shoulder holster beneath his jacket, and cautiously knelt beside the suspect checking for a pulse. Slightly relieved as the first patrol cars arrived on the scene along with a medical unit from the local fire station, Bob suddenly thought of his partner again. Feeling guilty to have forgotten him, he turned to look for Anderson in the turmoil, but he was nowhere to be found. When he finally caught a glimpse of his partner, a smile tugged at the corners of his mouth. There, back behind the temporary crime scene line, hastily erected by the first officers on the scene, Andy was standing quietly with the attractive blond leader of the Girl Scouts. She had just finished writing something on a small piece of paper, which he took and placed in his wallet.

Chapter 18

Some 1,450 air miles northwest of Seattle and 335 miles south of the Arctic Circle on the southern coast of Alaska lays the port city of Anchorage. With relatively moderate winters and mild summers the population of one of the world's most strategic locations rocketed from 48,000 in 1970 to nearly 175,000 by the end of the decade. Basing a major portion of its economy on the exploitation of natural resources, especially oil, had brought Anchorage more than its share of loners and seedy characters looking to make a quick buck, not to mention both men and women of rather questionable backgrounds seeking to use the remote location to escape the searching eye of the law.

Northeast of Anchorage, off Interstate 1, nestled in the Matanuska Valley of south-central Alaska in the shadows of the Chugach and Talkeetna mountain ranges, is the small community of Palmer. A throwback to the early '40s and '50s, Palmer, with a main street lined with shoddy bars and a local clinic that cared for the people from miles around, was a place where no one looked out of place. The inhabitants of Palmer, at least those who worked, commuted to Anchorage and the surrounding small villages. The rest were unemployed, on welfare or just transients desiring an inconspicuous place to hide out until the time was right to move on. What better place to blend in and disappear, for as long as necessary, than this isolated Alaskan community whose people tended to mind their own business.

As the afternoon stretched into evening, the plane and two of its passengers moved closer to their final destination. It had been just over three hours since they left Seattle. Nora, sensing his evil mood, sat staring at the magnificent Canadian and Alaskan coastlines as it passed below them, while Johnny struggled quietly with his dilemma. He had come so far only to make a mistake even an amateur would not have made. Now he must risk a contact to correct that error. But what was life for him now anyway? Wouldn't every day be a risk for him? Why not one more? His decision made, he relaxed momentarily and ordered a drink.

As the plane began its final approach over Cook Inlet toward Anchorage International Airport, Nora peered out through the window on a beautifully clear summer evening. The landscape below was spotted with giant oil rigs that ran one after another along the Kenai Peninsula. Within minutes the plane landed on the runway and taxied to the main terminal where the passengers departed.

Johnny and Nora remained seated until most of the passengers had left the plane. Then he took her by the hand and led her cautiously down the ramp. As they walked into the gate area, his eyes scanned the crowd frantically for the slightest sign of trouble. When he was convinced they had succeeded and were out of any danger, a smile crept slowly across his face. He had done it! Now all he needed to do was tie up one loose end.

They walked to the baggage area and picked up the luggage Nora had hastily packed for both of them. As they started for the door to catch a cab, Hardy stopped.

"What time did you tell your sister to pick up the van?" She glanced at her watch and figured the time difference.

"Sometime early in the evening. Why?"

"I need to talk with Joey. Where would they be now?"

"I suppose at Mom's house." Nora's voice showed signs of concern. "What's going on? What's the matter?"

As if he hadn't heard her query, he took her arm and walked to the nearest phone. "Call your mom now."

Her mother answered the phone on the second ring.

"Mother, this is Nora," she said, pausing momentarily then glancing at Johnny. "Are Patty and Joey there? Put Patty on the phone, will you. No, Mom, nothing's wrong. Hello, Patty…no, no, nothing's wrong. Hold on, will you?" She handed the phone to Johnny.

Placing his hand over the receiver he told Nora to take a short walk, then turned his attention toward the phone.

"Patty, put Joey on the phone."

Their conversation lasted about two minutes. When he was through, he hung up and met Nora outside, where she had wandered with the baggage. She didn't appreciate being left out of whatever was going on and she took that opportunity to let him know it. He laughed at her brazenness. She had learned more than he realized while he was away. He explained that it was just some business that he didn't want to bother her with, and then brushed her off by patting her on the butt and hailing a cab. When the cab pulled up at the curb, they got in. He leaned over the front seat and said to the cabby, "Chilkoot Charlie's," and the cab sped off.

The cab left the airport on Spinard Road and took a left on Minnesota Drive heading north. When it reached West Northern Lights Boulevard, it turned right and two blocks down stopped in the parking lot of Chilkoot Charlie's, one of Anchorage's toughest nightspots. Nora paid the cabby as they stepped out into the cool summer air. She had taken the time while on their flight to go to the bathroom and remove her bra. She hoped that she could distract Johnny from what was bothering him. But that never did happen. Now as her breasts felt the crisp air through her white silk blouse her nipples protruded noticeably without any recognition from him whatsoever. Johnny walked to a pay phone in the foyer of the building and dialed a number that he had memorized a long time ago.

Long fiery arrows of light pierced the tattered makeshift curtains and danced across the deeply furrowed brow of the man on the sofa. As the light crept slowly down across both eyes, he stirred momentarily and then slipped back into a deep sleep. Suddenly he was shaken from his perch by the pealing of the phone propped up next to his pillow. Frank Alanzo fell to the floor, banging his elbow on the dilapidated pine coffee table where his lit cigarette had burned to a nub in the ashtray.

"Shit," he mumbled to himself as he reached up and grabbed the phone. "Yeah."

"Frank, is that you?"

Slowly regaining his senses, the sound of a familiar voice from the past shook him.

"Hardy, is that you?"

"Who the hell else do you think would be calling you in this godforsaken place?"

"Where are you? When did you get out? Or maybe I should ask how?"

"You don't want to know. We're at Charlie's. I'll explain everything when you get over here and get us."

"We? What's this we shit?"

"Later. Just get your ass down here and pick us up."

Alanzo hung up the phone, still not quite believing his own ears. He pulled his five-foot-ten-inch pot-bellied frame off the floor and walked to his room to get a shirt. The last time he had heard, Hardy had been put away for quite a while. He remembered years before Hardy had told him that if he ever needed a place to hide out until the heat cooled down, he would high-tail it up to his tiny four-room cabin located off the beaten track in an isolated area just north of Palmer. And now here he was. He wondered what the hell had happened and how he had gotten out. And who was this other person. Hardy's never had a partner, per say, a lot of friends and acquaintances but never anyone he would trust as a partner. Well, he would find out soon enough. He threw on his coat, jumped into his jeep, a necessity in this area, and sped off toward Charlie's.

Chapter 19

Opening the front door of Charlie's, he was immediately engulfed in a white cloud of cigarette smoke. As he waded toward the bar through the crowd of men and women, he noticed the naked dancers scattered throughout the crowd performing their sexual treats on the eager money-laden patrons, many of whom worked in the oil fields. Over the last two years, he had been in town less than a dozen times and those times were only for supplies. The cops wanted him too and because he valued his freedom more than anything else, he had very little time to worry about coming to places like this. Besides, there were women in the community that catered to men like him, and on more than one occasion, they visited his four-room cabin for the evening. Lately, he had become acquainted with a lady in town and they had developed not only a physical but also an emotional relationship that seemed to meet both their needs for the time being.

Just then he caught sight of why he was there. Sitting at the bar on a stool was the unmistakable silhouette of Johnny Hardy. Even with the buzz haircut, it was Hardy. As he approached Hardy, he noticed the shapely woman sitting beside him. Assuming it was one of the local hookers that had hit on him, he ignored her and approached him. Just before he reached the stool, Hardy spun around, stood up and looked down at Alanzo. For the first time in a year and a half, a huge grin spread across Hardy's face.

"How the hell are ya?"

"Why you…" He paused as the Asian beauty that was seated beside Johnny spun around in her seat and stood next to him.

"It's OK. She's with me."

"So I see," Alanzo said slowly stroking his chin. "What the hell is going on? How did you get here? The last I heard you were still in jail and scheduled to stay there for quite a while. And who's the girl?"

Johnny laughed out loud. "Slow down, will ya? I'll answer one question at a time. Let's have a beer and I'll explain everything to you."

The threesome found a booth in the back corner of the crowded bar where they could expect some privacy and Johnny proceeded to explain his situation to Frank. After their third beer, he finished and waited for Alanzo to speak.

"Holy shit. You gotta be hotter than a pistol after target practice. We gotta get you someplace where you can hide out till the heat cools off." Then thinking another second he continued, "If the heat ever cools off."

Chapter 20

By the time Joey got to 25th and Jefferson, the area had returned back to normal. The linen truck used by Nora and Kruger had already been discovered less than a block away and had been impounded by Seattle police and taken to their recovery lot for evidence processing. The door-to-door search for witnesses, done in the area around the recovered truck, had ended hours before with little or no results. He had taken the bus to the Capitol Hill area from the University District and walked about five blocks to where the van was parked. He opened the door, which was unlocked, and got in. A seasoned veteran when it came to dealing with the police, Joey already had a story prepared in case the van had been staked out by the cops.

He placed the key in the ignition and delayed turning the van on for a moment. When he was sure that there would be no surprises, he started the van and pulled out onto 25th. As he headed down the hill toward Interstate 5, he continually checked the rear view mirror for a tail or any other sign of a problem. When he was sure he was not being followed, he got on the freeway and headed for the Sea-Tac Airport.

When he turned onto the third floor of the parking garage, all of his senses immediately kicked in. His head pivoted back and forth, not only in an attempt to locate the van, but also to scan the area for the cops. He already knew how dangerous this might be. If the cops had Johnny's getaway van staked out and he drove up and got in, he knew there was a distinct possibility that he would not get out of the van alive.

It took him about ten minutes, but he finally spotted the van. Not wanting to rush and be careless, he decided to drive around the lot two more times just to be sure he hadn't missed anything. By the time he returned to Johnny's van after the second time around the lot, he had decided he would take the chance. He pulled up behind the van, put on a pair of work gloves he kept under the front seat, jumped out of his van and slid open the side door of the getaway vehicle. Once inside the van, he quickly pulled the Ruger from beneath the refrigerator, tucked it under his shirt and hurriedly got out of the van. He slid the door closed quickly, jumped back in his vehicle and drove out of the lot and down the ramp to the pay booths. He quickly paid the attendant then headed out of the airport toward Seattle.

When he talked to Johnny earlier, he told him to dispose of the gun somewhere in Puget Sound, the body of water lying east of Admiralty Inlet, through which ocean waters reach inland some fifty miles from the Pacific Coast. He had considered getting on the Bainbridge Island ferry and tossing it off the ferry halfway across, but as he drove north on the freeway he decided that what Johnny didn't know wouldn't hurt him. He pulled the gun out of the waistband of his pants and placed it in the glove box of his van, inadvertently sealing both his and Johnny's fate forever.

Chapter 21

After a short stay in a local clinic to help him recover from his self-induced malady, Johnny settled down to a quiet and peaceful life in Frank's little cabin outside of Palmer. It didn't take long for Johnny to settle in and feel comfortable in his new surroundings. But after about a month at Frank's he was getting cabin fever and needed to venture out and see the opportunities the back country could provide him. Besides, his heroin craving as well as Nora's were much more than Frank's contacts could provide for.

His first stop was the small town of Palmer; but after scouting out the town he was definitely of the opinion that this was not the best place for him to continue his calling. With such a small community it would be difficult for him to pull a job, or for that matter even to score some additional drugs, without the eye of the entire community being upon him. So, as his daddy had always told him, "Don't crap in your own back yard." He would venture out a little farther and hope for better fortune.

And venture out he did. Within the first six months of his arrival in Palmer, there were over a dozen armed robberies and several large burglaries in the surrounding towns and cities that he, Nora and Frank pulled off. They wouldn't make him an instant millionaire, but they certainly kept all three of them in their much-needed heroin, which, thanks to another connection Frank had made, was never at a shortage. However, the good times they experienced in Palmer were short-lived. After a series of unlucky robbery attempts and several stupid mistakes on their part, the police were quickly narrowing their investigation much too closely to Palmer for Johnny's comfort. One night after several beers, Johnny confided his thoughts to both Nora and Frank.

"I think it's time we pull up stakes and get out of this area."

"Where would we go?" Nora questioned.

"I'm not sure yet, but any suggestions would be appreciated."

Frank look across the table at Johnny with a sorrowful look and said, "I sure hate to leave this place. It's been good to me for a long time. But I guess you're right. With the cops getting closer, pretty soon not even Palmer will be a safe haven."

"I say we head south toward the lower forty-eight and see what happens. Besides, your connections in town seem to be drying up. If we don't find another source soon, we'll all be in trouble."

"Are you crazy?" Frank blurted. "You know what's waiting for you down there. And if the cops ever get wind that you're back, you might as well pull the trigger yourself."

This hit a dreadful note in Nora's mind. She couldn't bear to be without him again, especially permanently. Was she willing to take that chance too? He was right about one thing. If they didn't find a better source soon, none of them would be worth a plug dime. Reluctantly she said, "What happens if we return to Washington? You know Joey is the best source of heroin you could ever find, but the risks are pretty great. Frank's right. If the cops get wind that you're back in the area..." She stopped as her eyes filled with tears as she was caught in the emotion of what she was suggesting.

"Well, I guess we just better not let that happen." He smiled at Nora then reached out and grabbed her hand. "I won't let that happen. We'll be safe enough for a while. Once we set up a supply chain with Joey, we can get out of town and head south. How's Arizona sound?"

She squeezed his hand and nodded with a smile, not wanting him to know how she really felt.

"You're both nuts, but what the hell. What's life without a little danger? I'm in!"

The next morning the trio packed up their belongings. Before leaving town, Frank made a call to his girlfriend, Linda, and persuaded her to travel with them. The three left Frank's cabin for the last time and headed to Palmer where Linda lived. When they arrived, Linda was waiting for them. Once they placed her small suitcase in the car, they were off and running for the States.

Chapter 22

Why had he returned? Frank was right; it was insane, even though it had been over a year since his hasty departure. To think that a craving for one substance could be so great that it could control your entire life. But here he was, eyes strained and bloodshot, head throbbing with pain, as he struggled to seek out an avenue of travel should it be necessary to make a hasty escape. Then he crept as steadily as his shaking limbs could carry his tall sinewy frame through the nighttime shadows, lest someone should recognize his face and place him in the area again. As he reached the car, an older model dark-green Chevy Nova, he paused briefly to look around and make sure he hadn't been followed. Convinced he was alone, he opened the door and got into the driver's side.

Waiting alone in the car for the past thirty minutes was Nora's brother-in-law, Joey Martinez. Joey had come from LA where he had an assorted police record from petty theft to armed robbery. To Johnny, Joey's marriage to Patty Chin, Nora's sister, had been a stroke of luck. Joey was a member of one of the LA street gangs recently expanding its membership to the Northwest area, thus increasing the accomplices he could now choose from, and it just so happened that the gang was also one of the Northwest's major black-tar heroin distributors. This gave Johnny an easy source to an endless supply of his much-needed panacea.

As Johnny entered the car, Joey was nervously running his dark fingers over the barrel of a Colt .357 Python that Johnny had picked up cheap from a friend of a friend.

"What the hell are you doing, man? You want to get us busted before we even do this job?" Johnny chided as he reached over, grabbing the gun from Joey's hands, and stuffed it under the front seat. "Both of us don't need these things." He reached under his pea coat and withdrew a .38 caliber revolver from the waistband of his faded jeans. "Your job is to keep your eyes out for the cops and I'll take care of the rest. You understand?" he said as he tucked the gun back into his waistband. Joey shook his head but still wasn't convinced that this job was worth the risk.

Johnny peered out at the dark evening. The sky was clear, unusual for this time of year, and there was just a little sliver of moon affording them the darkness that they required. Both men sat huddled in the Chevy for another half-hour without talking. In this older residential side street in the north end of the city, there were no house lights on, so both men felt confident that their presence had been undetected. Slouched down in the front seat of the car, he felt as safe as he could be at the time. He glanced up into the rear view mirror, scanning the block behind the car. He was turning away when he first noticed the silhouette of a car with its headlights off moving very slowly down the street toward them. He watched and waited. It was the unmistakably silhouette of a marked police cruiser, probably the local patrol officer making a routine check of the darker back streets of his district. Without a word, both men sank even lower in the front seat of the car. As they did, Johnny removed the revolver from his waistband once more. There was no doubt in his mind what he would do if happened upon by the unsuspecting officer.

Joey's eyes widened with fear as first anticipation and then panic ran through his body.

The squad car slowed to almost a complete stop one car length behind them. The interior light went on and Johnny could see the officer, car radio in hand, as he wrote something on a pad located on a clipboard balanced between the steering wheel and the bulky winter coat the officer wore. Was he there on a call from some suspicious homeowner who might have been alarmed by two strange men sitting in their car? Was he recording the license plate number on his pad while at the same time checking the plate with his dispatcher? If so, it wouldn't take him long to retrieve the information on the Chevy, stolen two nights ago in the south end. Johnny's right hand gripped the gun tighter as his left hand moved slowly toward the door handle. He knew that once the radio dispatcher forwarded the information over the radio, officers who worked adjoining areas would soon be there to assist him, thus reducing his odds of escape even more. He cursed himself and swore that if he got out of this one that he would never forget the handheld scanner again. If he was to take action, it must be now! He would have the element of surprise on his side.

As if responding to a statement made by Hardy, Joey sensed the danger they might soon be in. He reached over and grabbed Johnny by the coat as if to say, "No man, count me out!" It only took a second for Johnny's maniacal response. It was something that even Joey never expected. With the quickness of a leopard, Johnny turned in his seat, grabbed Joey by the throat with his left hand and with his right hand thrust his gun into Joey's open mouth. Before he could do another thing, the patrol car's headlights lit up the inside of their car. Instinctively, Johnny released Joey's throat and turned to exit his car toward the officer in the cruiser. What happened next surprised even Johnny. The emergency lights of the patrol cruiser went on and the car made an abrupt u-turn and sped off westbound on an emergency call.

His adrenaline still pumping, Johnny glared back over at Joey who, still slumped in his seat, was frozen with fear from the unexpected actions of Hardy.

"If you ever try that again, I'll kill you!"

There was no doubt in Joey's mind that Johnny was capable of carrying out his threat. He was still gasping for air as Johnny replaced the gun in his belt. He knew this wasn't the time or the place to confront this crazy man, but he swore that there would be a time someday when this man would pay up for his humiliation tonight. For now it was better to continue with what was planned.

When the patrol car disappeared, Johnny took a black wig from a paper sack in the back seat of the car and placed it on his head. He then removed some dark makeup from the same bag and began applying it to his face. When his makeup job was completed, he handed the bag to Joey and told him to use the makeup on his own face. Reluctantly he took the bag from Johnny and put on some makeup. Then both men got out of the car and started walking eastbound along the narrow roadway. When they reached the intersection at Greenwood Avenue and Holman Road, they stopped outside the perimeter of a streetlight and surveyed the area. The restaurant, less than half a block east, stood alone against the backdrop of one of the cities oldest residential areas. A local Chinese restaurant, it had the reputation as a place where one could find an excellent but inexpensive meal, as well as a friendly illegal card game now and then. This reputation meant plenty of unrecorded cash flowing through the owner's hands most nights. In Johnny's irrational way of thinking, there was no reason why some of the cash couldn't flow through his hands and eventually through his veins.

He opened the ornate wood-paneled door and entered into the front of the restaurant while Joey slid in behind him and slowly moved to his right against the large plate glass window that overlooked the intersection and the restaurant parking lot.

Johnny's hand gripped the small revolver tightly inside the pocket of his black pea coat. With heightened irritation, he approached the owner who was busy writing something at the cash register. As he approached, the dark-haired Asian man behind the counter seemed to anticipate a problem and backed up slightly. Luckily, there were very few patrons in the restaurant that evening. Most of the business was in a separate bar room area adjacent to the register, which was visually screened off by an eight-foot by twelve-foot wall colorfully decorated with the logo of the restaurant. Johnny removed the gun from his pocket, extended it toward the small man and ordered him to open the till. The man, trembling as he reached for the register, tried to assure him that he was welcome to anything he had in the till. Unfortunately, his pigeon English did nothing but irritate Johnny even more. Hardy ordered him to place all the money from the till in a paper bag he had produced from the other pocket of his pea coat. The man removed what few bills there were in the till and handed the bag back to his assailant. When Hardy looked at the contents of the bag, the expression on his face turned from anger to wild rage. Where was all the money he had expected to find here? It certainly wasn't in the till. *Maybe the chink kept it on him,* he thought. He ordered the man to empty his pockets into the bag. As he began to comply with the orders, an employee exited the bar room and walked behind the counter unaware of what was happening. His first inkling that something was wrong was when he felt the butt of the gun crash down on his head. As the employee fell to the floor, Joey moved to the front door, sensing that it was time to make their exit. To his horror, Johnny, for no apparent reason, opened fire on the man standing at the register, striking him once in the right shoulder. When he hit the floor beside the other man, Johnny wildly fired three more shots into both of their bodies.

With the sound of the first shot, Joey bolted out the front door in the direction of their car. As the door slammed closed behind him, three more shots rang out followed by a short pause. Then the front door burst open and silhouetted the tall thin body of a wild man, gun in hand, coming through the front door of the restaurant screaming uncontrollably like a banshee straight out of hell. By the time both men reached their car, Johnny had regained his composure, tucked the gun back into his waistband and had already discarded the pea coat and black wig in the nearby dumpster. Without speaking another word, both men wiped the makeup from their faces. Johnny reached down and started the stolen car with the two wires protruding from the ignition and they drove off southbound on the main road as the first patrol car, responding with lights and siren, passed them northbound, never giving them a second glance.

Chapter 23

The County Police Department held its roll calls prior to the start of every shift. Today was no different. When he arrived at work that evening, he was handed a memo by the shift supervisor saying the CO wanted to see him after shift in the morning.

"What happened now, Bob?" questioned the shift sergeant as the night crew slowly crept into the roll call room.

"Be damned if I know. It's been months since my last citizen complaint. Besides, says right here, he wants Andy too; he must figure I'll confirm his illicit sexual behavior on and off duty." Turning to his partner he said, "Hey, partner, you been jilting any more waitresses lately?"

With his right hand held high in the air, left hand deftly tucked in behind his back with his fingers crossed, he said, "I swear, Bob, I haven't even as much as dunked my donut!" Then hesitating for a moment he thought again and said, "But, umm, all those sticky buns!"

The roll call room erupted with laughter as Andy, who loved the attention, relived his recent culinary conquests.

After a few minutes of unbridled remarks, the shift sergeant regained control of the roll call room and commenced with the vital information for that evening's activity. After assigning individual uniformed patrol officers to their patrol districts, he directed his attention to the plainclothes units and their respective assignments.

"McCall and Baker, I want both of you up in the north sector of the Adam One district. Barnes has been getting his ass kicked with car prowls. Take the van, stay off the main roads and get into some of those small residential areas. If you have to, set up shop on one of the less-traveled side streets and see what you run into."

"What's the time frame, Sarge?"

He began, "According to our Crime Analysis Unit—" then was interrupted by an unidentified officer.

"Yeah, the pussy posse," came a loud shout from the roll call room, alluding to the office staffed with all female officers.

Evidently perturbed, the sergeant continued, "According to Crime Analysis Unit, between one and four in the morning. So don't let me catch you guys napping or out to coffee during that time."

"Napping? Coffee? What gave you that kind of idea, Sarge?" groaned Baker. "You've hurt our feelings."

"I was born at night you two, but not last night. Just make sure your butts are out there when they're supposed to be." Unable to continue the hard-ass routine he smiled and turned back to the rest of the troops.

"Bob, as for you and Andy, its Friday night and God knows what kind of a night this is going to turn into. For now, I want you two in the south end of the Adam districts along the strip. Bob, have you got your scanner with you?"

"Yeah, sure, Sarge."

"Good, keep an ear out for anything going down in the north end of the city. The supervisor for Seattle's North Precinct gave me a call tonight. They're a few men short. If anything serious goes down, I want you two to use your judgment in responding to back them up. If you do, don't forget to have dispatch let them know you'll be in the area in plainclothes. I'll be at the precinct finishing this damn scheduling, so keep me informed over the radio." He continued, "Any questions? OK, that's it. Let's hit the streets. And for cryin' out loud, be careful out there."

As the uniformed officers finished loading their patrol cars with the items essential for their survival, DeNucci, in jeans, an old pullover sweater and red wool vest, and Anderson in Calvin Kleins, a wool-lined jean jacket and tan cowboy hat, jumped into their unmarked police cruiser, a brown Dodge four-door sedan, and sped out of the precinct parking lot.

Andy spoke first. "What the hell is it about the brass and these sedans anyway? Somebody's got to be getting a kickback on all these. The whole idea of having a plainclothes unit was being inconspicuous. How inconspicuous could you be in a standard police-issue cruiser? It seems as though every dirt bag in the area knows what type of car we have."

"Oh well, just another hurdle to overcome in the day of a crime fighter," Bob quipped jokingly.

Both laughed as they headed out to what they hoped would be the hottest call of the night...coffee! Little did they know a long night had just begun.

"What do you think the old man wants with us?" Andy asked quizzically.

"For once I've got to say he's really got me stumped," replied Bob.

They traveled the side streets from the precinct through adjoining Lake Forest Park, an incorporated area within north King County, and finally wound their way around to Aurora Avenue North, the main thoroughfare through the Adam districts on the west side of the precinct. They turned off Aurora Avenue and into the Denny's parking lot on N. 155th, ten blocks north of the Seattle city line.

"The last time he talked to me was about a month ago, right after the shooting," Bob continued as they pulled their sedan into the last parking spot in front of the restaurant. He turned off the car and both men walked silently into the restaurant.

"Hi, guys," shouted the busty little redheaded waitress as they entered. "Follow me." She led them through the hustle and bustle of a Friday night restaurant crowd to a booth in the back where most of the officers that frequented the restaurant preferred to sit. It was both private and inconspicuous and it kept both the obnoxious drunks and the meddlesome customers from spoiling their coffee breaks or dinner. She seated both of them, poured their first cup of coffee and left with a smile and a promise to return for refills.

Bob immediately took his cup and sipped the steaming dark liquid, while Andy added cream and sugar before indulging. Then Bob continued the conversation from the car.

"He just walked right up to me in the hallway outside the sergeant's office, shook my hand till it hurt and said, 'Good job, hell of a good job,' and that was it. That's probably the only thing he's said to me in the year he's been at the precinct."

Counting silently on his fingers, Andy replied, "Yeah, well, that's seven more words than he's said to me in my whole career. And now he wants to see both of us tomorrow?"

Captain Randal Barnett was known to his troops as a man of few words...when he wasn't talking, and that was all the time. He was known to the current administration as a short-timer, or a man with just a few months left until retirement. When he was transferred to the precinct last year, rumors of catastrophic proportion had preceded him. According to officers in his previous command at the south-end precinct, the man was a virtual one-man demoralization squad. He was a complete and utter workhorse, and micro-managed every operation, major or minor, that went on within his command. He never gave his front line supervisors any slack in supervising their men. He had the knack of totally breaking down the morale of his men and supervisors, and to the dismay of the supervisory staff, shortened the chain of command to one man—himself. He hounded his men day and night until the very mention of his name caused ulcers. This fanatical egotist had forced three of the best supervisors in the south precinct into early retirement.

But things changed during this, his suspected last year of a thirty-year career. He was happy in the south precinct. He built his reputation there and, for all intents and purposes, considered that precinct his *home*. He was commander there for almost ten years. Then, for some unknown reason, some paper-pushing asshole (as he so lovingly referred to the pinheads that spent their careers at police headquarters downtown), decided he would spend his last year exiled away from the home he had built and molded to his taste. This was too much for his ego to take. So instead of Old Blood and Guts Barnett bursting through the front door of the precinct on his first assigned day, what the shift supervisor received was a phone call from a tired old man who said he was sleeping in that morning, and would he notify him if something came up? From that day on, the shift supervisors had the run of the precinct while Captain Barnett sat in his office, crossword puzzle dictionary in one hand, eagerly awaiting the day he could pull the pin and retire. He spoke only to the shift supervisor on duty when necessary and his secretary when he needed coffee.

"So why now," Bob muttered to himself. But before he could answer his own question, the alert tone on his pocket scanner beeped three times. The tone was an alert to all officers monitoring that frequency that an emergency was being dispatched. As he removed the scanner from his shirt pocket and placed it on the table in front of him, he noticed that the small red light over the city police's frequency was lit.

"And we're off," joked Anderson with a smile and a final gulp of his coffee.

Chapter 24

"All west side units...We have a report of multiple shoots fired at the Lotus Blossom Restaurant located at Holman and Greenwood. Suspect description to follow."

As the description of the two suspects was being broadcast, both Anderson and DeNucci were up from the table and on the way out to their car. As they headed toward the front of the restaurant, Bob placed a couple of dollars on the front counter and motioned to the waitress. "We'll be back, keep it warm." Then they disappeared through the door into the night.

Bob started the car and backed out of the parking space as Anderson hurriedly removed the blue "Kojak" light from its magnetic mount on the floor of their car and attached it to the metal plate that was bolted to the dashboard of the car. He turned the light on as the sedan sped out of the lot and onto the main highway southbound toward the incident. Anderson opened the glove box where the police radio was mounted and grabbed the microphone.

"David 67 to radio."

"Go ahead, 67."

"Would you advise the supervisor we are headed south into the city to assist city PD with a call of multiple shoots fired at Holman and Greenwood."

"Ten-4, David 67."

"Does Friday night always have to start this way?" complained Anderson as they wove in and out of the heavy traffic.

"Only in certain professions, Andy my boy, and this happens to be one of those certain professions."

As DeNucci continued to weave in and out of traffic trying with all of his driving skills to avoid the late-night drunk or an unconcerned motorist, Anderson concentrated on the broadcasts coming from the small portable scanner he now held in his hand. Once more Anderson picked up the car radio.

"Radio, advise Seattle units we will be responding in plainclothes in an unmarked unit."

"Copy, David 67."

As the unmarked sedan sped across the city line, that same uneasy feeling he had experienced a month before on the night of the shooting, crept back into DeNucci's mind. Call it intuition or anything else you'd like, Bob DeNucci had experienced it long enough to realize that he and his partner were about to get into something that was bigger then either of them expected.

As they rounded a bend in the road the spotlights of patrol cars three blocks away illuminated the area around the restaurant. DeNucci pulled their car in behind one of the marked units. Both men scanned the area and made individual assessments. They notice that along with the usual pile-up of patrol cars, a K-9 unit had begun a track west from the restaurant.

Before they exited the car, Bob said to Andy, "Why don't you contact the supervisor and see what other info they've got. I think I'll tag along with the K-9 unit and see what he turns up."

"Alright, don't forget your portable," Anderson replied as he tucked his own radio into the waistband of his jeans. "If you need anything just give me a holler."

Before they got out of their car to join the hunt, both men took the time to attach their police ID and badges to the outside of their jackets, lest one of the patrolmen at the scene not familiar with the duo mistook them as the suspects. As Bob stepped from the warmth of the car, he immediately felt the unusually cold air bite the skin on his face.

"You pick up anything yet, Casey?"

Casey Meed looked up from the track his dog had just begun and recognized the man in plainclothes.

"He's pickin' up good indications westbound from the restaurant along the roadway. We can't be more than ten minutes behind whoever was here."

"We heard you were short tonight, you want some backup?"

"Don't mind if you do. Even with my partner's good nose, things get pretty hairy out here in the dark. Besides, from what I hear from Union One's initial contact at the restaurant, the shooter sounds a little crazy. I mean, you know, yelling and screaming."

"Just consider your back covered," Bob assured him as he joined Meed in a jog behind the dog.

Meanwhile, Anderson contacted the supervisor and the first officer on the scene, and was being briefed as the medics worked frantically on both victims.

"Seems to me that we've got a couple of crazy dopers runnin' around out here," the uniformed officer told Andy.

"What gives you the impression they're dopers?"

"Well, when I arrived, one of the victims was still conscious. He was rambling on in Chinese, so I got hold of one of the cooks to translate for me. The victim gave him a description of the suspects and then told him that when this guy who shot him reached over the counter to take the money, he saw several track marks between the guy's fingers. I'm told by some of the other patrons that the kid should know what he's talking about because he's a doper himself."

"Are you saying that the shooting was drug-related?" Anderson asked as he jotted down notes in a small notebook he carried.

"Hard telling with these people; the Chinese are pretty tight-lipped. I don't think there's a lot we're going to get from any of them."

Anderson shifted his attention toward the two victims now surrounded by a team of paramedics who, despite the cold weather, were perspiring profusely as they frantically attempted to stop the bleeding from the victims' wounds.

"What do you think? Homicide or assault?" Anderson quizzed one of the paramedics.

"The young one took a slug in the shoulder and one in the hip. He'll live. The other, we're unsure of right now. We'll probably know a little bit more when they get him to the hospital."

The K-9 unit was still heading west about four blocks from the restaurant when the dog seemed to lose the track on the suspects.

"Damn it, that's what I was afraid of," Meed said disgustedly. "It seems as though our two friends must have gotten into a car somewhere in this general area and took off."

Lights were now coming on all over the area and the people began peeking through their blinds and curtains.

"If it's all the same to you, Casey, I'm going to do some bell-ringing and snoop around a bit. Maybe someone saw these two and they don't realize it." DeNucci left the K9 team and walked up to a residence whose lights had just come on.

"While you're busy playing policeman, I'm going to backtrack with the dog and see if we can find anything we overlooked the first time."

DeNucci, out of breath from running behind the dog, made a mental note to get out and do more jogging, then trudged up the front steps of the quaint brick Tudor and knocked on the door. Immediately the door opened halfway and a middle-aged woman wearing baby blue lounging pajamas appeared.

Meanwhile, Meed and his canine partner, Magnum, retraced their steps and were one block east of where they lost the original track. It was there, in the parking lot of a small apartment complex adjacent to the street, that Magnum once again picked up the scent. The dog, now on a tether with his handler close behind, made a beeline for a large green dumpster located in the corner of the parking lot. Meed released the dog from the tether and removed his .9mm automatic from his holster. The dog was now giving clear indications that someone or something was in the dumpster. Carefully, the handler called back his partner. With flashlight in his left hand and pistol in the other, he approached the dumpster. On the side of the dumpster, facing out toward the open area of the lot, was a three-foot square metal door with a latch on the right side. He placed his back firmly against the dumpster just to the right side of the door. With his gun poised in an upward position at shoulder height, Meed reached over with his left hand, opened the latch and threw open the door. As the metal door slammed against the other side of the dumpster, making a loud metal clang, he instinctively held the flashlight out away from his body, so as not to silhouette himself when he lit up the left side of the dumpster. With a quick turning movement of his head toward the open doorway he could determine that the left side was empty. Unwilling to allow his partner to jump through the dark opening, not knowing whether a mad man was inside, he did the next best thing. In one quick movement, Meed rotated his body in a low crouch away from the side of the dumpster, light held high and gun pointed inward facing into the center of the open doorway. Then, completing the rotation, he threw his back up against the opposite side of the doorway and checked the right side as he had checked the left. When he was satisfied that the dumpster was empty, he relaxed slightly and signaled

Magnum to his side. He now made a more exact inspection of the inside of the dumpster with the beam from the flashlight and found what Magnum had keyed on.

He always believed that perseverance paid off, no matter what line of work you were in. So he wasn't the least bit surprised when on the twelfth set of steps he was forced to climb, he hit pay dirt. The old man who responded to his knock had rumpled gray hair and a thick gray mustache to match. Dressed in his nightclothes, as everyone else was at this time of the morning, the old man's attitude quickly changed after he identified himself. He invited DeNucci in. Not wanting to seem ungrateful, he accepted the man's hospitality and sat down on a small badly worn divan in the front room of the house. The old man reached for his dark-rimmed glasses perched on a small table, placed the glasses on the end of his huge red nose and plopped down in a billowy red armchair next to the divan.

"What can I du fer you den, Mr. Officer?" he said in a thick Norwegian accent.

Politely Bob said, "We seem to have had a problem in the neighborhood this evening, sir." But before DeNucci could finish, the old man responded.

"It wouldn't have to du wit dose young fellars parked in front of my house a little while ago in dat brown or green Chevy, would it?"

Bingo! "Well, matter of fact it might, Mister...?"

"Peterson, Pete Peterson," he replied.

"Well, Mr. Peterson, these men that were parked out front, did you get a look at them?"

"Ya, sure, I was sitting right here den in dis chair about an hour or two ago. I don't get much sleep dese days so I take a sleeping pill and I have to sit around and wait fer it to work. So I come downstairs and sit right here in dis chair in da dark until I feel like going to sleep." He paused to cough and catch his breath. "Two young fellars. Da first one, da driver, he got out right away and he walked up da block." He pointed eastbound. "Da utter one just sat in da car. I couldn't see him too good because it was pretty dark in da car, but dat fellar dat got out, well he was a long drink of water with not much meat on his bones. I'd say maybe six-two. He was wearing a dark pea coat. Kind of hung on him like a scarecrow." He hesitated. "You know, I could have sworn he had light brown hair."

"In the dark I'm sure it was difficult, Mr. Peterson."

"NO, no, you don't understand. Dis first fella came back in about a half-hour and got back in da car. They both sat dare for quite a while. Den dey got out. Dis is what I don't understand. When da big fella got out da second time, his hair was jet black and pulled back into a ponytail. I yust can't figure dat one out."

"What about the second man?" Bob asked

"He was Mexican, dat's for sure. You know dey all sorta look alike, dark skin, dark hair. But dat's all I can say about him. I was so puzzled about da otter one."

DeNucci scribbled furiously on a note pad he had taken from his shirt pocket. When he finished his notes he asked if there was anything else Mr. Peterson could remember. When Peterson told him he couldn't remember anything else, he thanked him, excused himself politely and headed back toward the restaurant.

Andy had just finished talking with the sergeant when the first city detective arrived. The door on the dark green Dodge swung open and Detective Kelly Egan, all six foot five and 275 pounds of him, lumbered out of the car and onto the crime scene. The big Irishman, with the face of a leprechaun, massive long arms and tree trunks for legs, extended his thick paw toward Andy with a smile.

"Hey, Andy. Top of the morning to ya."

Andy's unusually large hand disappeared within the grip of the Irish giant. He was sure glad that they were on the same side.

"Hello, Kelly," he said and grimaced from his vise-like grip. "Why did you pull this one tonight? I thought they had you stashed down in the south end of town running down burglars?"

"They did until tonight. All the big boys on the homicide and robbery squads are either working a case or off on vacation. So guess who gets stuck with the leftovers?" He laughed at his own joke, then herded Andy and the sergeant toward the restaurant.

Egan was no stranger to homicide and robbery investigations. For ten years he had been one of the finest homicide and robbery detectives in the entire city department, with an arrest and conviction record that still had not been beaten. His problems began only after the commander of his unit, and a personal friend and rabbi of his, decided it was time to retire. The new boss hadn't looked on Egan's accomplishments in the same light. Instead, he burdened him with dozens of bullshit cases; the type which up until that time were considered to be unfounded or with no viable suspect. This, of course, caused him to waste hour upon hour on futile attempts to solve cases that either didn't occur or were at the low end of the solvability scale. Within six months he had worked on more than one hundred of these cases, substantially delaying his progress on any of his major caseload. In turn, his new boss now had the excuse he needed to transfer him back to the precinct and promote one of his own cronies, a cruel fact of life in police business. But Egan had taken it in stride and had joked about his ability to make "lemonade out of lemons." Still tonight's case assignment was a chance for him to get back in the chase and he was going to make all he could of the situation.

Chapter 25

Meed placed his gun in his holster, reached up with his right hand and keyed the switch on the microphone attached to the collar of his blue fatigue uniform.

"K-9 seven to Command Post."

"Go ahead, K9 seven," the voice of Kelly Egan boomed.

"My partner and I tracked the suspects westbound from your location and lost the track about four blocks away. It looks as though they got into a car at that point. We doubled back on the track and located what I believe to be a secondary track. We're now three blocks due west of your location in the parking lot of the..." he paused, "the Sunset Apartments. I think you ought to send an evidence technician to my location."

"Ten-4 K9 seven. Say, is King County, David 6, with you?"

"Negative. I left him back at the end of the first track. He decided to check some houses in the area for witnesses."

"David 7 to David 6."

"Go ahead. 7," Bob replied as he walked down the cement porch steps leading to the sidewalk.

"Did you come up with anything. Bob?"

"Matter of fact, more that I expected."

"Good. Why don't you head east to the Sunset Apartments. The K9 unit located something he wants us to look at. I'll see you there in a few minutes."

By the time he arrived at the apartments, Anderson and Egan were both crowded around the open dumpster.

"What! Is it lunch time already? What did you find? Some old corn beef and cabbage?"

"It's lunch time alright and it's your turn to buy. asshole," Egan replied with a grin as he turned and once again held out his hand. "Long time no see. How's my favorite wop?" He continued in a thick Irish brogue, "You still married?"

"I am, but I'll never know why she's stayed so long." As they shook hands, he realized how small he felt next to this giant of a man. "What did we find?"

While Egan gently stroked the head of the German shepherd he replied, "Well, Meed here and his partner seem to think they've stumbled upon some important evidence. Why don't you take a look and tell me what you think."

As DeNucci looked through the dark opening, he shot an arrow of light over the contents of the dumpster. Now he realized why Mr. Peterson had become confused. There at the rear right side of the dumpster on top of the daily garbage was a black pea coat and black wig with a long ponytail. He then relayed his conversation with Mr. Peterson to everyone at the dumpster. One of the uniformed officers present shook his head.

"Shit," he blurted. Then grabbed his radio, "Union 1 to radio."

"Go ahead, Union 1."

"Did you get a response on that plate that I ran just before that aid call you sent me on?"

"Stand-by, Union 1."

"You sure he said a brown or green Chevy with two people aboard?" he asked DeNucci.

"That's exactly what he said."

"Just before I received an aid call, I was running a plate on a Green Chevy Nova just west of here."

"Union 1, was that plate UHU167?"

"That's affirmative."

"Union 1, is that vehicle occupied?"

"Shit, I knew it, shit!" he muttered to himself. "It was when I last observed it, radio."

"Union 1, we have a 10-61 on that vehicle. Stolen out of the south end. Do you have that vehicle, Union 1?"

"Shit!" he said disgustedly to everyone there. "Negative, radio, I do not!"

Chapter 26

With sirens howling in the background, they continued southbound from the restaurant. But Joey wasn't listening. As he gazed out the passenger side window of their car, he could feel the knot in his stomach turn to nausea. He hadn't planned on this. His wife had warned him earlier about Johnny, but they needed the money so he had gone along with him. Now, not only had they robbed a restaurant but also that crazy bastard had shot two people. Worst of all, they only got a hundred and twenty-five bucks, hardly enough to split between them, considering the habits they both had. And now maybe a murder rap. His body visibly began to tremble uncontrollably. Suddenly, he felt a hand tighten around his left arm.

"Pull yourself together. If you blow this whole thing now just because you don't have the balls, I'll blow your fuckin' head off. You understand?" He shook his arm violently and Joey shook his head like an obedient little puppy then turned and stared out the window.

They had driven about five miles south when suddenly Johnny pulled off the road into a shopping center parking lot.

He parked the car in a garage adjacent to an all-night grocery store. Then with a disgusted look, he turned to his brother-in-law and spoke.

"Get out of the car and take any crap that belongs to you. Don't leave anything behind. And lock the door."

Joey did what he was told and nervously waited for Johnny, who had remained in the car. Johnny retrieved the revolver he took from Joey earlier. He placed the gun in his waistband along with his own gun. He pulled a blue cable-knit sweater from another paper sack in the back seat of the car and put it on over the flannel shirt he wore, careful to cover both guns. He turned around in his seat and conducted a last-minute check around the inside of the car, and then out he came.

"Let's go," he commanded Joey. "Before anyone realizes, we'll be resting at home in bed." He had a connection in a local chop shop, and in a few days when the heat died down, he would take the car there and trade it for a "colder" car.

He headed off eastbound and Joey followed right behind. He didn't know why he followed him through the dark city streets other than for safety. As they walked silently through the darkness that surrounded them, he swore to himself that once they were out of this, he and his wife were splitting. He wasn't going to be humiliated one more time by this son-of-a-bitch. He would…In the middle of that thought Johnny abruptly stopped in mid-stride. Joey, worried that somehow the police had found them, began to retch violently. At the sound of Joey's first gag, Johnny spun around on the balls of his feet and struck him square on the face with the back of his hand, knocking Joey to the cement sidewalk, where he remained, bleeding from a cut on his cheek.

Johnny had no room for weakness in his plans. Not if he was to continue living in freedom. That was enough of this pathetic creature. Leaving Joey sprawled on the cement he bounded across the street to where an old tan Pontiac was parked. Using a small tool he retrieved from his rear pocket, he jimmied the side window and within a minute was in the car. After another minute of jostling under the steering wheel, the car started. Within seconds, he was driving off down the street and disappeared, leaving Joey heaving uncontrollably on the sidewalk.

Chapter 27

He got back to the precinct after five that morning. Even for a Friday, it had been exceptionally busy. By the time he got home and into bed with his wife it was past six a.m. Another hour and she'd be up with the kids getting them ready for school. As he drew the covers up he reached over, patted her on her soft bare thigh and then passed into oblivion.

When he awoke, startled by the alarm clock, it was nine a.m. He dragged himself out of bed and struggled across the room to the shower. He quickly dried and wrapped a terrycloth towel around his waist. The bathroom door opened and his wife appeared with a hot cup of coffee to greet him. As he grabbed the coffee from her left hand, he felt her other hand brush across his chest.

"Thanks, hon. I hope I didn't wake you this morning when I got in."

"No, you didn't," she said. "Too bad." The shapely brunette untied her robe, and they both laughed as his towel fell to the floor. He pulled her close to his wet naked body and kissed her passionately.

"Just hold on there, big fella," she said teasingly. "Breakfast is getting cold. Besides, Andy just called to remind you that you have to pick him up at 9:45. That gives you enough time to shave, dress and maybe finish another cup of my delicious coffee before you leave."

She turned and left him there in a most uncomfortable state. He watched as the shapely figure that was hidden under the robe and in his hands just seconds before left the room. Hypnotized for a second, he suddenly snapped back to reality and walked back to the sink to shave.

Fifteen minutes later he was rushing down the stairs, holster and revolver in one hand, reaching for the hot travel mug of coffee his wife was offering at the front door. She patted him on the butt, gave him a quick peck on the cheek and pushed him out the door. "Don't forget, Andy," she said playfully, knowing quite well that it would be the last thing he would forget.

He wondered if he could remember to pick up something special for her this afternoon before he came home. But for right now he had another question on his mind that wouldn't be answered until he picked up Andy and saw the boss.

When he arrived at Andy's apartment, he honked twice. Seconds later Andy appeared at his second-story balcony and signaled that he would be down in a minute. After several minutes of waiting, Andy came racing through the front door of the apartment complex and got in the truck with Bob. As he left the building, a cute redhead in the apartment above his came out through the sliding glass door onto her balcony and hung over the railing in her red satin bathrobe waving frantically.

"Don't forget about dinner tonight, Andy," she sighed as her God-given attributes flowed from the front of her loosely tied robe.

Andy returned her reminder with a smile and a promise to be there by six. Then, looking thoroughly rested, he turned to Bob and said jokingly, "To the office, James."

"Don't forget about dinner tonight, Andy," Bob mocked in a voice three octaves higher than his own.

"Some guys just don't know when to quit." He looked once at Andy and then took one more look at the vivacious redheaded siren dangling loosely over the railing, put the car in gear and drove quickly away from the apartment, shaking his head.

Ten minutes later they pulled up to the eight-foot chain-link fence surrounding the precinct parking lot. Bob rolled down his window and punched a six-digit code into the electronic lock box. As the large gate slid gently back along its track on eight-inch steel wheels, he inched his truck forward into the parking lot and found a spot. The two men entered the rear door of the precinct and went directly to the captain's office where the captain's secretary, the effervescent Anne Hollingsworth, was there to meet them.

Anne had been the receptionist at the precinct since she graduated high school, ten years ago. Although touted to be short on brains while endowed with a body that would put a Miss America to shame, Anne Hollingsworth was as they say, *"Dumb as a fox."* Nothing occurred at the precinct, or for that matter in the department, that got by Anne. For that reason, Anne was a well of information if one knew how to tap it. And you could count on the fact that many a man had tried although very few could claim to have succeeded.

"Hi, guys," she said in a familiar tone." He's not in yet, there's still time for a cup of coffee if you want."

"Cream and sugar for me," said Andy. "Bob takes his the way he likes his women: hot and black."

With a shrug your shoulders phony look of disgust, Bob looked first at Andy and then back to Ann.

"Don't worry, Bob. I don't believe a thing he tells me."

"Well, if that's the case, you're the only one," he commented as Anne left to get them their coffee.

Both men seated themselves comfortably on thick cushioned office chairs that the old man had brought with him from the south end.

"Let me handle this when she gets back," Bob told Andy.

"Why you? Don't you think my animal magnetism will open her up?" Andy pleaded.

"We don't want her *opened,*" Bob said in mocked disgust, "we just want some information. Besides you heard what she just said. She doesn't believe a word you say," Bob finished as Anne returned with the two coffees.

"Now let's see, who gets what? You boys always get me so flustered."

They both retrieved their coffee from her desk, knowing that the dumb act was just a routine she had gotten into. *She may not be the brightest bulb in the pack,* thought Bob, *but there was no better source of information in the precinct.* Everything that went on here, in one way or another, passed right through her hands and ears.

Bob thought the direct approach might work.

"Anne," he said," how about lunch with Andy and me this afternoon?" Andy, caught totally off-guard, choked on a swallow of coffee and excused himself from the office to clean up the mess he had just made on the front of his jacket.

He waited for Andy to leave the office and then continued. "I mean, that is, after our meeting with the captain." He caught himself smirking. "What would be so important that he had to have us in here first thing in the morning?" The trap baited, he sat back to see if the prey would snap at it.

"I don't know, Bob. He got a call from Major Gregory yesterday, but it was a short one," she smiled. "It couldn't have been that important."

"Gregory. What the hell does he want?" he pried a little more.

"You know, Bob, I'd tell you if I knew, but the captain has been totally close-mouthed about all this."

Bob knew that was a lie. If the captain was going to speak with anyone about anything that was to go on in his precinct, she would be all ears at the door getting as much information as she possibly could. He also knew from experience, once Anne said she knew nothing, there wasn't anything that could be offered that would change her mind. So at least now they knew the boss talked to his good friend Gregory, and Gregory was the man in charge of the Major Crime Investigation Unit downtown. He knew by her posture that she knew more than she was telling, but she wasn't about to give it up, yet.

When Andy returned, he could tell by the look on Bob's face he hadn't gotten very far.

"Time for a little magnetism," he whispered to Bob as he walked past their seats and behind Anne's desk chair, where she sat busily shuffling papers the captain would need to see when he arrived. He extended his arms and with his strong hands, began to message Anne's soft and silky shoulders. Quickly she relaxed, removed her glasses and leaned back in her chair, placing her flowing brown hair firmly against his mid-section. The more he rubbed the lower she sank in her chair and the higher her knee-length skirt crept up her lap, exposing among other things, her surprisingly long and shapely bare thighs.

Suddenly, without warning, she sprang forward out of his grip, grabbed her glasses and frantically pulled at the skirt that had already exposed more than most men had ever seen. When Andy looked up, he was staring into the frowning brown eyes of the old man himself.

Captain Barnett stood poised against the door to his office. DeNucci, with his back to the door, realized immediately what was happening when he saw Andy's face and turned to face the captain.

"I trust you gentlemen were enjoying yourselves this morning? I'm not interrupting anything, am I?" he said in a tone less than menacing.

"Er...no, sir," replied Andy as if he were the proverbial cat caught eating the canary.

"Sorry I'm late. I'll see you in my office now." As the two men entered the office behind the captain, Bob reached over and slapped Andy on the back of the head.

"Way to go, ace!"

Once inside the office, the captain closed the door for privacy. But Bob and Andy both had seen Anne switch on the captain's intercom before he arrived that morning. Nothing was sacred or safe around this place.

"Sit down." The captain motioned for both men to pull their chairs closer to his highly polished mahogany desk piled with paperwork.

"You both know, as does everyone else in this department, that in less than six months I'll be pulling the pin and retiring. When the brass downtown wants you to go, they're not very subtle in how they tell you. Well, contrary to popular belief, there's still some life left in this old bastard. I've been taking notice of the exceptional way in which you both have worked together. Aside from some minor reputations," he glanced toward Anderson and for the first time the corners of his mouth turned up into a smile, "you have compiled some impressive statistics. You're both a little unorthodox in your methods, but what the hell; you get the job done and from what I've seen you get it done pretty well. That's why when the Major Crimes Division called me the other day and asked me to recommend two officers from our plainclothes unit to fill two detective vacancies, I recommended both of you." He reached over and opened the top drawer of his desk. He withdrew two gold detective badges and tossed them across the desk at both men. "As of nine o'clock Monday morning, you're both reassigned to the Homicide and Robbery Division. Any questions?"

Neither man knew what to say. They just sat there dumbfounded and stared until Anderson asked, "As a team?"

"Yes, God help them…as a team!" The smile returned to his face as he looked at DeNucci.

"And God help the women of the county. Do you think you can control him?"

"Doubtful, sir, very doubtful, but I'll give it a try."

"Well then, get the hell out of here and go get prepared to give your new boss ulcers."

Both men rose from their chairs holding their newly acquired badges in their hands and walked out of the captain's office into the reception area where Anne awaited them with a smile.

"Now wasn't it better that I let him tell you rather than spoil your fun?"

"Anne, you wench. I knew all along you knew. Thanks." Bob kissed her on the cheek.

Andy sidestepped his partner, grabbed Anne around the waist in a bear hug and swung her around. Anne squealed like a pig, while Andy smiled as he crushed her large breasts against his chest.

"You'll never change, will you?" said Bob.

"Never, never, never!" he replied.

"I hope not," Ann exhaled as he placed her back on the floor.

As they walked from the office, both men thought of what their new position offered. Bob thoughts centered on the regular time he could now spend with his family in the evenings, just like most other fathers. All those years of shift work had put a strain not only his marriage, but also on his kids, who for most of their lives had grown up with one parent. He had been like the proverbial ship in the night, just passing them on their way out to school in the morning or kissing them goodbye as he walked out the door to work when they returned from school in the afternoon. Monday through Friday, 8 to 4, weekends and holidays off, that is, when they were not on call. And best of all, a boost in pay. *Not a lot, but maybe just enough,* thought Bob, *to prevent his wife from having to return to work when the kids were in school.* This would be the perfect surprise for her.

Now Andy, on the other hand, had a whole different take on things. As he strolled down the precinct hallway, he was mentally calculating just how many dates he could line up for all those nights he was going to be available.

As they walked toward the men's locker room at the precinct, they heard the captain yell in annoyance down the hall, "Anderson, keep your paws off of my secretary. I'm not ready to lose her yet."

Chapter 28

It was 7 p.m. that evening when DeNucci received the page at home. As he looked at the number displayed on his pager, he knew what it was about. For the past five days he and Andy had been temporarily assigned to the Green River Task Force investigating the serial killings of over twenty prostitutes in the airport area. The investigation had lingered on for over three years and the task force had eliminated hundreds of suspects. Many of the officers had begun talking among themselves saying that all signs pointed to someone in or related to the law enforcement community. As of yet, this was strictly an inside thing between officers and some of the supervisors on the task force. No one was willing to come out publicly and express that feeling. (It would be almost twenty-five years before they would arrest and convict the suspect, not involved with law enforcement, in almost forty slayings. By then, most of the men currently on the task force would be retired or retiring…but that's another story.)

Today they would travel to the Olympia area, as they had for the last seven days, and keep surveillance on a suspect's residence. It wasn't really a clandestine surveillance. The suspect, a cab driver in Seattle, was well aware of the officer's presence twenty-four hours a day. As a matter of fact, on several occasions he had come out of his house, walked to their car and given them letters for the commander of the Major Crimes Unit. On one occasion he had led them on a high-speed frolic through the north Olympia area only to stop at a twenty-four-hour restaurant and offer to buy them a cup of coffee before they continued their chase.

Of course, the whole idea was to try to put some type of mental pressure on the suspect so he might possibly make a stupid remark or mistake and reveal something to the officers regarding the homicides. Bob and Andy both had known from the start that this guy was a few fries short of a happy meal, and doubted whether shaking a few more fries out of his bag would result in anything. But, orders were orders.

Today started out to be like every other day they spent in Olympia. A quick trip to pick up Andy and then a forty-minute race from North King County to the Olympia area (which normally took at least an hour of 60-mile-per-hour driving) to relieve the day crew. On the first three runs to Olympia, the State Patrol had stopped them a half dozen times for speeding. After that, they decided they would keep their Kojak light handy and plug it in every time they passed a trooper. Since that third day, they had not been stopped once.

Today, while in warp drive on Interstate 5 just south of the Tacoma Dome, an indoor arena located in Tacoma, Washington, often referred to as "The Woodshed," and the world's second largest arena with a wooden dome (only the Superior Dome in Marquette, Michigan, is larger), their day took an unexpected ninety-degree turn. It was Andy's day to drive and as usual, he spent more time glancing out the rear view mirror than he did the front windshield. But today Andy's habit was about to pay off. As they passed the Tacoma Dome, Andy glanced at the car behind them in his rear view mirror and instinctively began to slow down.

"Hey, Bob, check that out," he said as he motioned to the rearview mirror with a head gesture.

As Andy moved into the far left lane, Bob checked out the car behind them through the passenger side mirror. The sun was just beginning its departure from the northwest sky, but there was still enough light to identify the car behind them as a green Chevy Nova, license number UHU167; the car used in the robbery and shooting at the Chinese restaurant a few weeks earlier.

"Well, well, what do ya know," Bob said as he now focused all his attention on the green Nova rapidly gaining on them.

Andy backed off the gas and the green Nova sped by. Bob reached down and grabbed the Kojak light and placed it on their dashboard. The moment the blue light exploded through the windshield of their car, both officers knew they were right. The Nova hit the gas and began swerving in and out of the southbound traffic in an attempt to evade them. Bob picked up the radio, advised the dispatcher what they had and asked her to contact the State Patrol for assistance. Moments later the dispatch advised him that the troopers were responding from south of Olympia and would attempt to cut the suspect off if he got that far.

As the two cars raced in and out of traffic at speeds in excess of ninety miles per hour, baggies of white powder thrown from the driver's side window exploded in puffs of smoke as they hit the pavement.

"We've got a live one, Bobby."

"Yeah, just keep your eyes on the road," said DeNucci as he checked his seat belt, "or we may not be among the living very long. This asshole is crazy."

"What's the update on the State Patrol?" Bob picked up the radio and checked with dispatch.

"They're about ten miles south of your location. They're planning on shutting down the freeway at Yelm, one exit south of the bridge."

"OK, dispatch, we'll meet them there."

Suddenly, without warning, the Nova hit the brakes and screeched to a halt on the shoulder of the roadway. The driver threw opened the passenger door, slid out onto the shoulder and jumped over the small guardrail barricade into the brush on the side of the freeway.

Anderson was quick to react. He hit the brakes and in a four-wheel drift, followed the Nova onto the shoulder of the freeway. DeNucci, half out of the car before it stopped, hopped up on the guardrail and catapulted himself down the small ravine onto the back of the fleeing suspect. He would later thank his wife for the jeans and long sleeve shirt she suggested he wear that day. Without them, the thorn bushes and underbrush would have made shreds of his arms and legs as he tumbled down the gully with the suspect in a headlock. Both men ended up in a heap at the bottom of the gully where DeNucci remained in control. After alerting dispatch of their location, Anderson caught up to the two and assisted Bob with cuffing the suspect and dragging him back up the hill to their car. By the time they got the suspect back to the freeway, the State Patrol officers had arrived and were closing down the inside lane of traffic to assist in their investigation.

The suspect was cut and bruised on both arms and the bridge of his nose had been broken in the fall he took when DeNucci bulldogged him to the ground. He was a white male in his late thirties, long blond hair and a full beard. By all accounts, he did not fit the description of any suspect the officers had. *So how,* Bob thought, *did this dirt bag fit into the puzzle?*

Chapter 29

As they sped back northbound on Interstate 5, the two officers talked casually to the suspect, now identified by his license as Charles (Chuck) Castle. Castle, handcuffed and seated in the rear seat of their patrol car, asked one of them to reach in his top shirt pocket and get him a cigarette. Bob reached back over the front seat, and grabbed the crumpled pack of Luckys nesting in his shirt pocket. He removed a cigarette from the pack, placed it in Castle's mouth and a few moments later lit it with the car lighter. Then he placed the pack of cigarettes back in the suspect's shirt pocket and waited.

Castle was a current two-time loser for auto theft, with a rap sheet that spanned thirty years of misdemeanors and felony crimes. After his first puff, he looked up at Bob and shook his head.

"Shit! I knew I shouldn't have left town today. Man, that was only cut I had in the car. There was no shit in those envelopes. I just got scared when you turned on your light and I started throwing them out the window."

Both Bob and Andy knew that this guy was blowing smoke up their butts. But they knew they had him by the short hairs. They weren't interested in the cocaine charge. What old Chuck seemed to have forgotten was that he was a two-time offender. If convicted of a third felony this would be his third strike, and, according to Washington state law, he would be going away for some time. So both men knew it was open season on Chucky.

Bob reached back and pulled the cigarette from the suspect's mouth.

"It sure was luck that you spotted that Nova, partner." Bob winked over at Andy.

Andy, picked up on the hint and continued, "Yea, you think this guy is the trigger man or the driver?"

"What da ya mean trigger man?" asked Chuck quickly.

"What do you mean, what do I mean?" said Andy. "What do you think I mean? Why do you think we chased you anyway?"

Castle had the look of a deer in the headlights. "Uh…I was speedin'?"

"No, dirt bag! The car you were driving is stolen."

"Oh well, Officer, I…I didn't have any idea."

"No idea at all?" Andy continued.

"No way. Why I bought this car, oh about two weeks ago. And I've even been stopped before this and no one's ever said anything."

Bullshit, thought Andy.

"So you bought it two weeks ago? Great!" Then turning to Bob he said, "I guess we got ourselves the shooter!"

"Shooter! No way! I ain't done nothin' like that. You got the wrong guy."

"Well, that's funny. You said you bought the car two weeks ago. You didn't report it stolen at any time you owned the car and last week this same car was used in a robbery and shooting in Seattle. And now guess who's driving it today?" Andy witnessed a transformation of expression on the suspect's face from bewildered to horrified. He turned away for a second to relieve the pressure of the smirk that now went from ear to ear. Looking over at Bob, he silently mouthed the words *Got ya,* then let Bob handle the rest.

It took about fifteen minutes for Chuck to spill his guts. He was a middleman for a Seattle chop shop. Two days ago an old friend he hadn't seen in over two years had contacted him in Seattle with the green Nova. His friend, Frank, had shown up at his north-end apartment about 6:30 p.m. with some other guy named Tommy and two women—one white and one, he thought, was Asian. Frank had told him that the Nova they were driving was sort of hot and they needed a different car to get around. Normally he didn't do deals at his own place, but this other guy, Tommy, pulled out a wad of cash and offered it to him on the spot. He told them to come back in the morning and he'd see what he could do. They all showed up this morning at 7:30 and he swapped the Nova for a blue Ford four-door with all the proper paperwork and then they took off.

"We're going to need more than a blue Ford as a description, Chuck," Bob said.

"It was a blue 1975 Ford LTD. I don't remember the plates, but they were good. Oh yeah, it had some body damage to the driver's side rear panel, so the panel was replaced and it's gray now."

"So when you say they took off, where did they say they were headed?" Bob asked cautiously.

Chuck squirmed in the back seat. "Come on, man, I just ratted off a friend and told you what I do for a living. What the hell more do you want?"

"Everything or we head straight for your parole officer's office. It's your choice, man; you can either walk for the info or wind up in jail. Either way, we win."

"Shit, man, you really gonna make me screw over my friend?"

"Hey, Chuck, it wasn't my friend that put you behind the wheel of that stolen car and now on your way to jail." Now it was time to shut up and let him stew in reality.

Chuck sat in the back of the patrol car as it rushed northbound towards Seattle and his probable home at the King

County Jail. Then his parole officer would probably violate him, and back to the joint he'd go. That was not a high priority on his list of things to do.

"Gig Harbor," he blurted.

"Excuse me, Chuck, did you say something?" Andy shouted back over the sound of the radio blasting in the front.

"Lower the damn radio, will ya, man." When Bob turned off the radio, he spoke again. "I said Gig Harbor, man. They were headed for Gig Harbor. They were going to stay in a local motel and then check out the area tomorrow for some burglaries, see what they could get and then get out of town."

"Smart answers, Chuck; now let's hope that you're telling the truth."

"It's the truth, man. I swear it."

"We'll know soon enough whether you're lying or not. Remember we know who you are, where you live, and what you do. So don't think we're just going to disappear." Both men had a hard time controlling their expressions, knowing what was coming next.

"You'll see, man, you'll see. Now I gave you what you wanted, how about me?"

Hey, Chuck, we're men of our word," Andy told him. " You get to walk...this time."

Andy pulled the car off to the side of the freeway just south of Tacoma, got out of the driver's side and opened the back passenger side door.

"OK, you walk," he said as he peered into the back seat.

"Walk? Shit, man, we're still south of Tacoma. How am I gonna get home?"

"Chuck, Chuck, Chuck," repeated Andy, "you held up your end of the bargain, now we have to hold up our end. There are other options, you know. Besides, what the hell do you think we are...yellow cab? Out you go, buddy. If you start now, you could make it in a day."

Andy reached into the rear seat and unlocked his handcuffs. "Out you go, buddy."

Chuck reluctantly got out of the rear seat shaking his head. "Man, you're fucking with me. I told you what you needed, and now you're fucking with me."

Chuck, we're just doing what we promised. Would you prefer the option?"

Chuck shook his head and headed off down the shoulder of the freeway toward Seattle.

When Andy got back into the car he looked over at Bob and they both broke out laughing. "Now the fun part."

Bob picked up the radio and called dispatch. "Would you tell State Patrol that there appears to be a pedestrian hitchhiking northbound on Interstate 5 just south of the Tacoma Dome?"

Prior to leaving the scene they had checked Chuck for warrants. When he came back as positive for numerous traffic warrants, they knew they had an ace in the hole. That's when Bob talked to one of the troopers and informed him of what they had. Confident that they would get the information they needed, he asked the trooper to follow them northbound at a reasonable distance. He would let him know when he could swoop in and collect this piece of trash. When he replaced the radio he looked over at Andy and mockingly said, "Sure glad we checked to see if he had warrants. I wouldn't want him to tire himself out with such a long walk."

"He's going to be one unhappy camper," Andy grinned as he continued northbound on the freeway.

Chapter 30

"You know this could be a long night," Bob mused to Andy as they pulled into the driveway of the two-story split-level in suburban Federal Way.

"Yeah, well, I could use the comp time."

"No doubt, with that bevy of honeys you keep."

The brown split-level was the residence of Major Jack Gregory, their new boss. The porch light was on and a dim light from the downstairs recreation room shone through the white linen curtains. Because of the hour, Andy decided to knock softly rather than ring the bell. After a short wait, the front door opened to reveal Jack Gregory in plaid pajama bottoms and a white terrycloth robe, chewing on what appeared to be, a Cuban cigar.

"This better be good or both your asses will be back in uniform tomorrow," he growled as he let both men in and led them down to his office in the basement.

Although not very tall, Gregory was a formidable man with broad shoulders, graying hair and a pot belly he had acquired just recently. A more typical cop there could not possibly be. He was a veteran of Korea. He did not have a degree, but rather learned everything he needed to know from working the street.

He enjoyed civilians addressing him by his police title of "Major" and his men calling him "boss." (His friends, from the department only, called him by his nickname Dickie, but only in private). He wore Ray-Ban sunglasses day and night, had full squared-off sideburns (never tapered), ate doughnuts on and off duty and drank his coffee hot and black (milk, cream or sugar was for pussies). And, of course, he was divorced...nine times. To Gregory, police work was a way of life and he was always trying to live it to the fullest. He considered himself a *real cop* and measured his men by the standards he believed he set.

Since Gregory was in between wives there seemed to be no need to keep the noise down. But as they entered his office in the basement, they heard footsteps coming down the stairs behind them. Annoyed, Gregory pushed his way past both men back out the office door, but not in time to prevent the shapely body of Anne Hollingsworth, wearing nothing but a man's T-shirt, from popping into the doorway.

"Oh my! I guess this wasn't the right time, was it?"

"Never mind now, Anne, just go on back upstairs and I'll be there in a minute."

"See you later, boys," she giggled as she returned up the stairs.

When he returned his attention to the office, both Bob and Andy didn't quite know what to say.

"So what's the matter with you two? You never get laid before?" Finally a small smile came to his face and he said almost apologetic. "Look, she's a good-looking woman and I'm an available man...again."

Neither man made any attempt to hide the fact that they were surprised, but now they knew why Anne hadn't told them anything about the conversation she had overheard on the phone between the captain and the major. She hadn't really heard any conversation between the two; she heard it straight from the horse's mouth.

As they sat in two brown cushioned chairs across the desk from Gregory, they related the day's events that finally brought them to his door that evening. When they finished, Gregory sat for a moment chewing on the stub of his cigar.

"Not bad, not bad at all. I'd love to beat Seattle PD's ass to the arrest of these creeps. What do you want to do?"

Bob explained their plan to the major who listened intently. When he was done, the major gave them his blessing and showed them to the front door. As they left the house, Andy looked back through the storm door just in time to view Anne, silhouetted by a light at the top of the stairway.

Chapter 31

The light from a full moon bathed the otherwise unlit section of highway as the car sped south on Interstate 5 through the suburban community of Federal Way, Washington. Hardy knew that their money was running dangerously low, but he wasn't worried, at least not yet. He had gotten word from a friend of Frank's that Gig Harbor, a tiny little bedroom community at the base of the Olympic Peninsula, was real easy pickins. Just a day or two there and they'd have more than enough to last them for a while.

Frank reached up from the back seat and grabbed his shoulder. "How long?"

"About another hour. You hungry?"

"Shit yea, I'm hungry. We haven't had a bite to eat since this morning. Find us a hamburger joint or something will ya? I'm starved."

He exited the freeway at the Fife exit and found a McDonald's close by. As all four of them dined on burgers and fries, Johnny and Frank discussed their plans for the following day. Nothing elaborate, just case a few out-of-the-way neighborhoods. Pick the house most likely to have what they needed, kick in a back door, grab the loot (including food), and on to the next. They figured two or three good stops and they'd be set for weeks. No more discussion was needed. They finished up their meal and got on the road again. For the remainder of the drive to Gig Harbor, everyone was silent.

In less than an hour they arrived at a little out-of-the-way motel. The two men gathered what little belongings they had and carried them out of their car and into the room. Johnny had been careful to dump the car they had used in the robberies up north. Frank had known someone in Seattle who was willing to trade the car for the one they now had plus some cash. They were assured the Nova would go to a local chop shop. By now that car was part of a dozen cars in the Northwest. Nora found a coffeepot in the room and proceeded to make a fresh pot as Linda, Frank's girlfriend, used the bathroom to freshen up.

Frank had insisted on taking Linda with them when they left Alaska, and so far she had proved to be useful to them. On their way through Montana they needed some cash, so Johnny decided that a bank job was in order. Early on a Monday morning the winds had kicked up something terrible, and by the time the Nova traversed the pass going westbound, the gusts reached fifty miles per hour. As the car leveled off on the flatlands, Johnny glanced at the gas gauge. Seeing it close to empty, he decided the next exit would be their stop. The car left Interstate 90 on the first exit ramp they came to, and in a manner of minutes they spotted a Shell station at the entrance to a sleepy little town just east of Livingston, Montana. Once they filled the tank, they drove through town and found a small local bank branch suitable for their needs. The only problem, two doors down from the bank was a little café that seemed to attract the local sheriff. When the bank opened at 9:00 a.m., two sheriff cars were parked outside the café with both on-duty officers inside having breakfast. Linda, whose shapely body matched, if not surpassed, that of Nora's, had volunteered to distract the officers while Johnny and Frank went into the bank. Not only did she distract the two officers, she devised a plan to disable their vehicles while they were being distracted. While Linda did her thing for the two sheriffs, Nora was out in the parking lot jamming toothpicks into the door locks on their patrol cars, leaving the vehicle locks totally disabled, hence delaying any response by either sheriff.

Everything had gone smoothly. Johnny and Frank covered their faces with some makeup the girls brought with them and Johnny grabbed one of Nora's wigs from her small carrying case in the car. By the time the officers received the bank robbery call on their radios, both women had rejoined their men. Before both sheriffs realized they had been bamboozled and their car locks tampered with, Johnny, Frank, Nora and Linda were miles away.

Johnny thought it was a stroke of genius on his part to use the makeup and wig during the robbery. He knew that victims had a tendency to focus in on something about the suspect. He also knew that the stress of the situation caused many victims to see and relate things differently from one another, making the police's job that much more difficult in determining what the suspect looked like. He decided from then on that he would make the situation that much more confusing with his disguises.

The night in Gig Harbor was a fitful one for Johnny as he tossed and turned and on several occasions woke up in a cold sweat. When at last the morning arrived, the sun poked its head out from behind the low clouds, burning off the billowy sea of white mist that buried the entire town. Johnny jumped out of bed and woke the others. Anxious to get on with the day's work, he hurried everyone out of the room and back to the car.

"What's the hurry?" Frank asked him.

"I don't know. I just...I don't know, we just should be going." His senses had never failed him before, so why shouldn't he believe them now?

As they headed out of town they pulled through the drive-in at a local fast food restaurant and got coffee and breakfast sandwiches. Then, as if chased by some supernatural ghost,

Johnny sped south out of town to look for their first victim.

It wasn't five minutes after they left the motel that the unmarked cruiser slid up to the curb outside the office and DeNucci and Anderson got out.

Chapter 32

The first house they spotted on Roby Street, a brown tri-level, was set back in the tall pines with an almost invisible entrance for a driveway. As they approached the house, the faint barking of a neighbor's dog could be heard. Johnny pulled the car up to the attached garage and while the others remained in the car, he slowly approached the front door. He rang the doorbell. When he got no response, he knocked on the door. When he still got no response, he sauntered around the house, casually looking into any window he could to determine if anyone might be inside. Once he was sure that no one was home, he went around to the rear door, in this case the rear door of the attached garage, and kicked it in. Nonchalantly he repeated the same procedure on the inside door. Once inside and assured no one was home, he went to the garage door and opened it up so the others could join him. Inside the house all hell broke loose. Cupboards were opened and contents were strewn across the floor. Dresser drawers were emptied on beds and rummaged through. Closets were checked for compartments or safes and of course the entire house was searched for any weapons. While the men ransacked the house, the woman quickly located any female's dresser or closet and took their pick of whatever they needed that would fit, including jewelry, coats, pants, blouses, panties, bras, nylons, shoes and any other item they deemed necessary.

At the end of the spree when they exited the house, they had made a haul much larger than they thought they ever would. Several diamond rings, which would pawn for maybe ten cents on the dollar, over a thousand dollars in cash, numerous pieces of clothing, a VCR, portable TV, shoes and most important, a six-shot .32-caliber snub-nose revolver, holster, and fifty round of ammunition. Frank had found a large green suitcase in the garage and the four burglars loaded their booty into it and placed it in the trunk of their car.

Johnny turned around in the driveway, proceeded slowly out onto Roby Street NW and headed back toward Highway 16 south to leave the area.

Chapter 33

They drove through the area most of the night, stopping long enough only to grab a cup of coffee and use the bathroom. Their eyes were bloodshot and they were running out of motels. If they didn't find a clue in the next three or four motels, they were set on returning home and accepting the fact that they had been screwed by Chuck. He would pay if that were the case.

The next motel was a little fleabag just outside of Gig Harbor. Just the type of motel where you would expect to find every dirt bag in the area living. As they pulled into the motel lot, they were spotted by a black male carrying a duffel bag and headed toward a beater '77 Dodge van. The man stopped dead in his tracks and followed their progress through the lot. When the car stopped in front of the office, he quickly opened the van door, threw the duffel bag into the back and got into the van. As Bob and Andy entered the front door, they heard the van slam into gear and quickly head out of the parking lot northbound. Both men stopped and took a moment to look at the van as it left in a hurry. They had become so in tune to one another that each man knew exactly what the other was mentally making a note of. This had become a game to both of them. Later, when they returned to their car, Andy would enter the plate number and description of the van in the small logbook they kept, while Bob would write a detailed description of the subject. They developed these habit months before while conducting a long surveillance. Because they had experienced quite a bit of success in identifying suspects and persons of interest in a number of other situations, they had continued to develop their log. As they would both agree, you just never knew when something would come in handy.

The two men entered the lobby of the motel where the desk clerk, looking as though he had just awakened, looked up from the newspaper he was reading, belched and asked them what they wanted. Bob displayed his identification and proceeded to ask the clerk if he had anybody registered who was driving a blue Ford sedan. A few minutes searching the counter produced a registration card in the name of Terry Fox.

"Are they still registered?" asked Bob

"Nah, they left about five or ten minutes ago."

"Which way did they go?"

"Hey, man, I don't get nosy around here, if you know what I mean."

"Well, how many people were with him?"

"With him? Hell, there was no him. It was two broads that come in here and registered. They probably had their old men with them...but like I was saying, it ain't healthy to go nosin' into other people's business."

Bob and Andy left their cards with the clerk and went back out to their car.

"Just where I like to be," Andy said sarcastically, "a day late and a dollar short."

"Yeah, I know, Andy. But sooner or later their luck will run out. Let's just hope it's sooner."

Chapter 34

The Ford and its four occupants sped down the Interstate 5 corridor toward the Olympia area, where Johnny knew someone who would house them for as long as they needed. When they left the freeway, they headed eastbound into the rural area outside of the state's capital.

The three-bedroom split was located in a quiet residential neighborhood just north of the state capital in Olympia. There were homes on either side, but each building lot was oversized so that everyone had their own adequate space. The manicured lawn, chain-link fence, dark-brown cedar siding and overall rustic looks blended nicely with its rural setting. There was a clump of fir trees in the front yard towering over the entire neighborhood, and at the base of those trees there were several pieces of used lumber and some tools identifying the beginnings of a child's clubhouse.

It was after dinner when Johnny pulled into the driveway. He turned off the headlights, but left the car running (an old habit). He opened the fence gate and walked to the cement stairway that led to the front door. Before he could get up the steps, the wrought iron porch light at the top of the stairs flicked on. Johnny looked up at the screen door and saw the silhouette of a huge man. The door opened and the big man's hand was extended.

"They said you was out, but I never thought I'd see ya in this area again."

"Yea, well let's just say I'm passin' through." Johnny took the big man's hand and shook it. Then, motioning to the car, he asked if they could all come in.

"Sure, come on in. Hey, honey," he yelled up the staircase, "we've got company."

"Sonny" Gondolfo was not an educated man. He grew up in a little Italian section of the Bay area. His mother and father divorced when he was five and his father was in and out of jail since then. Because his mom was forced to provide for the family by herself, Sonny was left to fend for himself on many occasions. As a child he was tall and spindly and a target for all the bullies in the neighborhood. At thirteen, after years of beatings by the local toughs, he decided he was going to do something about it. He dropped out of school, got a job at a local grocery store and started going to the gym and lifting weights. By the time he was fifteen, Sonny was six feet tall and 195 pounds of solid muscle. At twenty he had reached his physical maturity at six-feet four-inches and 245 pounds. Needless to say he had no problems with the local toughs any longer. Unfortunately, Sonny fell in with the wrong crowd and soon followed in his father's footsteps. He met Johnny, as so many others had, while doing time with him. Johnny had taken a liking to him and when Sonny was released, they promised to stay in touch. So when Johnny needed a place to stay in the Olympia area, Sonny was the logical choice.

Sonny introduced his wife Maria to everyone. Then while Maria took the women downstairs to get them settled, the three men sat at the kitchen table. Sonny pulled three beers from the refrigerator, passed them out and sat down.

"What the hell are you doin'? I thought you'd a had more sense then to be comin' back here."

"Relax, Sonny, no one knows that were even in the area. Besides, we're just passing through."

"Passin' through to where?"

"Seattle," Johnny said with a smile.

"You crazy bastard. After what you did, you step one foot into that town and they'll blow your fuckin' head off."

"Yea, well they'll have to find me first. You know me. I know how to take care of myself."

The conversation soon changed to what Sonny had been doing and how his kids were.

"I'm doin' fine. I work as a mechanic and I make pretty decent money. Maria...she just got herself a new job as a receptionist at a dentist's office in town. And both kids are goin' to school and that's where they'll stay if I got anything to say about it."

"We just need a place to stay for a couple of days; any problems?"

"No, man, you know what them Mexicans say, me casa is su casa. For as long as you need."

The next day Johnny, who was normally an early riser, slept in. When he got up, everyone already had eaten breakfast and Sonny had left for work. He walked up the basement stairs to the kitchen where he grabbed a burnt cup of coffee from the coffee maker and sat down to talk to Frank.

"You up for work today?"

Chapter 35

The car pulled up to the service station and Sonny came out.

"What's up?"

"We need to borrow a car."

"What are you, crazy? I can't let you take one of these cars."

"Look, it's just for a few hours. No one will ever miss it and I promise we're not going to hurt it."

"If I let you take one of these cars, my ass will be in a sling."

"And if you don't let me take one of these cars, where is your ass then?"

"Say, man, are you threatening me? 'Cause if you are, you can get your shit out of my place right now and hit the road."

Johnny leaned out the window of the car and grabbed Sonny by the front of his blue coveralls. "I didn't come all this way to threaten you. Besides you know me, I don't exactly play fair." He looked into Sonny's eyes with that crazed look that Sonny knew all too well. He had seen it a dozen times before and it was an unlucky omen for anyone it was cast upon.

"OK. man, but just for a few hours. You guys gotta promise to get it back to me in a couple of hours."

"Not a problem. Sonny. Thanks, you're a hell of a friend." Johnny released his hold on the coveralls and Sonny walked back inside the service station. When he returned, he had a set of keys in his hands.

"Here, these belong to the white Chevy parked over there, on the side of the garage."

Johnny parked the Ford next to the Chevy and placed the keys in his pocket. Then, without a word, both he and Frank got into the Chevy and headed back onto the highway. On the way to the station, they had seen some upscale homes that they figured might be just what they were looking for.

They drove up and down the street several times before they decided which house they would hit. The house they selected was a two-story white and brown Tudor. It was the most secluded house on the block because it was set back and surrounded by an eight-foot green holly hedge. As was usual, Johnny pulled up into the driveway right next to the house. There was no sign of anyone being at home nor was there any sign of unusual activity in the neighborhood. Just before he got out of the car, Frank pulled the .38-caliber they had taken from the burglary in Gig Harbor from the waistband of his pants and placed it in the glove box of the Chevy.

"There's no need to be carrying this around right now," he muttered to himself.

Things were going just as planned. Johnny knocked on the front door and got no answer. Then he went around back and checked the sliding door on the back deck. When no one answered, he returned to the front and quickly kicked in the dark oak-paneled front door. What Johnny, in his haste, had missed, was a small, but significant sticker located on one of the rear windows of the house. It was a silent alarm sticker. The minute the door was kicked in, an alarm sounded in the monitoring office and the personnel called the police.

Johnny and Frank were in and out of the house within two minutes with cash, food and jewelry. When he finally pulled out of the driveway and away from the house, they missed the police by less than a minute. Later that same afternoon after they had dumped the proceeds of the burglary off at Sonny's house, they headed back to the garage to pick up their car. En route back, an officer on routine patrol spotted the Chevy, which by then had been reported by a neighbor as a suspect vehicle.

When the officer hit his lights and siren, Johnny hesitated for a moment to be sure that the cop wanted him and then pulled over to the side of the road. Knowing that they had the car with Sonny's permission and had already dropped off the stolen property, Johnny felt rather cocky as the officer walked up to the car and asked for the license and registration. That smug look on his face soon faded when he opened the glove box and out fell the .38-caliber revolver Frank stored there earlier that afternoon.

Immediately the officer drew his weapon and took two steps back from the car so he could get a better look at both men. Frank, noticeably shaken, swore and mumbled under his breath. Both men were taken from the car at gunpoint and arrested when the serial number on the gun came back as stolen from their Gig Harbor burglary. In the back seat of the Chevy, officers found Johnny's small sports bag containing a blond wig, some pancake makeup and several hats.

On the trip down to the station, Johnny didn't say a word; he just stared at Frank. Frank knew he had screwed up but couldn't do anything about it now. Normally, when a prisoner or prisoners arrive at the station, they were fingerprinted and interrogated. But because court was currently in session, the officers never got that far. Instead, both men were immediately taken to the local district court where they were arraigned.

Because Johnny was always prepared for the unusual, both he and Frank had false ID from Oregon, compliments of the Department of Motor Vehicles which had inadvertently left the driver's license blanks where they could be appropriated. Prior to arraignment, both men were checked locally on WACIC (the state warrant system) and nationally on NCIC (the national warrant system). Both came back with clean records. The arresting officer had a bad feeling about these two, but without anything to back it up, he couldn't do very much. So, almost as an afterthought, the officer sent a teletype to all state agencies with the information on the two suspects and the contents of their car when they were arrested.

Since Hardy could prove that the car was a loaner from the service station where Sonny worked and they feigned ignorance about the gun in the glove box, both men pled not guilty to possession of a stolen gun at the arraignment. Burglary charges were pending while the investigation continued, and over the objections of the officers and prosecutor they were released on bail. Johnny quickly paid the minimum bail amount and both men were released from custody. When they arrived back at the house that evening after having to hitch a ride all the way from court, Sonny was in a foul mood. His boss was at the station and answered the phone when the call came from the police about the Chevy. He had been fired on the spot, and if that wasn't good enough, his boss docked his last paycheck to pay for the cost of the Chevy being impounded.

Sensing it was time to go, they packed up and prepared to leave the next morning.

Chapter 36

Situated in the shadow of the towering Mount Rainier, Puyallup, Washington, the home of the Washington State Fair, was a rural community just southeast of Seattle. For decades it had been a small, quiet community outside the fervor of Seattle. But, with the recent growth of some of the country's manufacturing and technological giants like Boeing, Warehouser, Microsoft and Intel, the face of the community was rapidly changing. New housing developments sprung up around the town where farms once flourished and the city limits stretched further and further from the core of the community. As the town grew, it attracted new businesses and as the businesses were absorbed into the town, its appeal to the city folk grew greater. Along with the increase of population came the problem of crime.

This Tuesday was like many others. A light drizzle hung in the air for the third day in a row and saturated the roadways through town. Main Street was filled with a constant stream of cars with their lights on and windshield wipers flapping, making it difficult for pedestrians to cross the street between businesses. About 2:30 that afternoon the drizzle stopped and for the first time in over a week the area was blessed with a view of her majesty the sun. The unusual blast of solar heat quickly dried the streets and within a half-hour raincoats and parkas had been replaced by shirt sleeves.

Just west of town off Highway 512, Frank dropped Johnny and Nora at a used car lot. The lot, run by gypsies, was not known for its quality automobiles, but the selection they offered would suffice for what they needed.

Immediately Johnny saw what he wanted—a 1969 Plymouth Fury station wagon with simulated wood side panels and a trailer hitch. The windshield was cracked but as long as it was dependable he would buy it. Within minutes a salesman joined them at the side of the car. After a few minutes of haggling, a price was agreed upon. For a mere one hundred dollars, he could drive off the lot with the car. When Johnny broached the subject of the broken windshield, the salesman told him they would be responsible for replacing the glass, all he needed was a day. Johnny realized this was the perfect way to ditch the car after their little escapade. He agreed to pay the one hundred and asked if he could take the car now and bring it back later in the afternoon for windshield repair. The salesman agreed and Johnny paid him the one hundred dollars. No one would look here for the car, at least not right away. They could do the job, come directly back here, drop off the car and be on their way long before the cops knew what hit them. He paid the man the one hundred dollars, provided him with a phony Oregon driver's license, and then drove off the lot in their new acquisition.

At 1:30 that afternoon Johnny and Nora, in the Plymouth, met up with Frank and Linda, in the Ford, outside of Bonney Lake, a little town just east of Puyallup. Johnny didn't want Frank to come directly to the dealer when they dropped off the car, so he told him to wait at a little coffee shop up the road and they would meet them there. About three o'clock they split up and Johnny and Nora headed to Puyallup.

At 3:30 that afternoon Johnny walked into the Raggamuffin, a retail clothing outlet on E. Main Street. The clerk, who was talking to a visiting friend, asked him if he needed help. He asked where the leather jackets were and he led him to the back of the store where he tried several on.

From the first minute the clerk talked to him, he had a bad feeling. When Johnny walked out a few minutes later, he followed him to the door and watched him get into a brown Plymouth Fury with an Asian female and drive away. Walking back into the store, the clerk made a note of the Plymouth's license number on a pad behind the counter: Washington license GRU058.

A short time later, he saw Johnny walk slowly by the front of the store and mentioned to his friend that he thought the store was being cased for a burglary. A few minutes after his friend left the store, Johnny returned and asked him for help with some jeans. The clerk gave him a pair of jeans and Johnny started for the changing room. But, before he reached the room, he asked the clerk for a larger pair. When the clerk returned to the changing room with the larger pair of pants, Johnny had painted his face with some type of pancake makeup and came out of the room wearing a pair of leather gloves and a wig. He pulled a small-caliber revolver from his jeans and pointed the gun in the clerk's face. He ushered the clerk to the register where he removed all the bills, then asked about a safe. The clerk took him to the office at the rear of the store where there was not one but two open safes. Johnny rifled through the safes, removing anything with a possible value. When he was done he turned to the clerk and ordered him back to the front of the store. Once they got to the front of the store, he ordered the clerk to lock the front door, which he did, and then told him to grab all the leather jackets. He had him place the jackets in a stack at the back door and returned with him to the front where they repeated the process with men and women's jeans. When all the clothing was placed on the floor at the back door, Johnny bound the clerk's hands and feet with duct tape and put him on the floor.

As the robbery proceeded inside, Nora drove the station wagon around to the rear door of the store and waited. Johnny ordered the clerk to stay still and remain silent while he carried the clothing out to the car. After the last load of clothing was taken from the store, Johnny shut the door and got into the station wagon and Nora drove off. After a few minutes, the clerk managed to break the tape on his feet. He got up and headed to the front door where he signaled a customer waiting at the locked front door. The customer realizing what had happened, called 911 and the police arrived in a few minutes.

Chapter 37

The Plymouth sped west out of town on Highway 512 toward the little café where Frank and Linda were now waiting. During the ride Johnny had removed the wig and placed it into a paper sack. Then grabbing some moist towelettes they purchased at the drug store, he removed the makeup from his face. When the car pulled into the parking lot, Frank came out of the café and met Johnny. Then both men drove their cars behind the café where they could not be observed and Johnny, Nora and Frank unloaded the Plymouth's contents into the Ford. Once they were finished they would deliver the goods to a fence in the area that Frank had known for years and collect enough money to last them for a while.

Nora stayed behind at the café as Johnny got back in the car and drove to the dealer where they had purchased it a few short hours before. He left the car with the salesman, as they had previously arranged, and told him he would be back the next day, after the windshield had been replaced, to pick it up. The salesman then agreed to give him a ride up the road to the café. When he arrived he thanked the salesman and walked behind the café where he met Frank, Linda and Nora. As the sirens blasted in the background, the blue Ford turned westbound onto the highway and back toward Interstate 5.

They had been down in the Olympia area far to long for Johnny's liking. He had spoken to the others about returning to the Seattle area because of its close proximity to the drugs they so desperately needed. Frank and Linda agreed it was probably a good move, but Nora, who up until this time had not really voiced her opinion, finally spoke up against the idea.

"I don't think this is a very good idea," she said slowly. "You know the police would like nothing better that to get their hands on you and you seem to want to tempt fate far too much. I think we should head south as we had planned before we left Palmer. We can set up a source down there once we get to where we are going."

But against Nora's wishes, Johnny decided it was time to head back to the Seattle area. Frank already packed what few belongings they had in the car and when they reached Interstate 5, they headed north. Nora was extremely nervous and could not get the ominous feeling of bad luck from her mind. They drove up through Peirce County and into King County while Johnny racked his brain for a place to stay. Just as they entered the city limits of Seattle, Johnny remembered a place up in the north end where he would be welcome.

In the month that followed, Johnny, Frank, Nora and Linda settled into an old two-story home of an associate in the north Seattle area. The house, an obscure run-down leftover from the turn of the century, located on Aurora Avenue North just south of 80th Street, provided them with anonymity and the base of operation they would need for the upcoming months. During their first sixty days in the Seattle area, fifteen armed robberies and twenty-three business and home burglaries could be attributed to their presence.

Chapter 38

When the police arrived at the Raggamuffin, the clerk, noticeably shaken, was pacing behind the front counter smoking a cigarette. The first information given officers was the license plate number and description of the suspect's vehicle, which the clerk had wisely written down the first time Hardy had entered the store. The officer immediately broadcast the plate number and description of the vehicle and then continued to take the report.

The following morning, a detective checked with the Department of Motor Vehicles and got the name and address of the owner of the suspect vehicle. He drove out to the local residence and soon found out from neighbors that the family had moved to Minnesota about a month before. When he followed up with the neighbors he was able to get the new address for the family in Egan, Minnesota. He returned to his office and sent a teletype to the Egan Police Department requesting they contact the owner and determine whether they still owned the suspect vehicle. Within twenty-four hours he had received a response from Egan. The owner had been contacted and told them that he had traded the car in to a dealer in Puyallup prior to moving. The detective called the car dealer who verified that they had taken the car in as a trade over a month ago, but had wholesaled the car to a local used car lot within the last two weeks. Armed with the used car lot information, the detective contacted the dealer within the hour. When he arrived at the lot, he immediately spotted the station wagon parked behind the office. Cautiously he contacted the owner of the lot and found out the car had been purchased for cash a few days before. The dealer went back into his records and produced the sales information showing the name of the new owner as Tommy Jones with an Oregon address. In fact, the dealer told him, Mr. Jones was scheduled to come in some time today to pick up the car. He left it there a day or so ago to get the windshield replaced. The detective showed several salesmen the composite drawing of the suspect in the Raggamuffin robbery. Although it wasn't anywhere close to a positive identification, the salesman tentatively identified the composite drawing of the suspect as the person who purchased the car. The detective thanked the owner and salesman, gave them his business card and asked them to delay the suspect if possible and call him immediately if the man should happen to come for the car. But he knew from experience that would never come to pass. After getting the information he needed, he returned to his office and did the only thing he felt might be helpful in this case—he sent out a teletype to all surrounding police agencies. He knew there would be no arrest in Puyallup, in the near future, for this robbery.

Chapter 39

It was a week since their arrival in Seattle and, since then, they remained completely secluded in the old house on Aurora Avenue N. The only time they ventured outside was for food. It was Johnny who felt the most pressure from being cooped up inside the tired old mansion. He paced the worn wooden hallways daily until he just couldn't stand it any longer. He knew that if he were ever recognized in the city his days were numbered. But he was prepared to do whatever was necessary to remain free, even if that meant killing or being killed for it.

It was early afternoon on the eighth day when Johnny decided it was time to reestablish his presence in the area. Both Nora and Frank were uneasy about Johnny's idea. But he had already depleted his inventory of heroin and was beginning to crave that irrepressible urge once more. He made up his mind and they knew there was no changing it at this point. So, while Frank and Linda remained at the house, Johnny and Nora took off in the Ford and headed south toward Federal Way. He remembered a bank that he felt was perfect for their needs. But a lot could change in several years so he and Nora paid a visit to the bank that afternoon to make sure that it was still a viable target.

As they pulled up into the parking lot of People's National Bank, the first thing both of them saw was a red Wells Fargo armored car parked out in front of the main entrance. They parked their car and watched as one officer exited the rear of the truck and entered the bank carrying two large money pouches. Several minutes later the same officer exited the bank and returned to the truck where he disappeared into its belly. When the truck pulled away, Johnny and Nora left their car and walked into the bank.

They entered the bank lobby and saw a seating area to their left for customer waiting for loan officers. To their right was a row of five wood-grained desks, each with a blotter, some office supplies and a nameplate on their smooth shellacked tops. Currently there was only one desk in use. A pretty brunette sat behind the desk in a burgundy high-back swivel chair, rocking back and forth and bouncing her exposed nylon-covered leg while flirting with the uniformed security guard. On the far side of the building the vault was situated behind three teller windows. Johnny wandered around the bank as Nora walked up to the brunette at the desk and asked her for some information on CDs. She pretended to be interested as she listened to the information the young lady had to offer. After she gathered some brochures from the young woman, she turned and met Johnny by the door and they both left the bank.

"This is a piece of cake, baby," Johnny smirked. "By this time tomorrow they won't even know what hit them."

They returned to the house up north and Johnny filled Frank in on what his role would be the following day. Both women were eager to take part in the robbery, but Johnny shot that down right away.

"Not tomorrow. We can't take too many chances yet. The fewer of us there are the less likely for a mistake. And right now we don't want to make any mistakes."

With that decided, the two women sat dejectedly in the kitchen and left the men alone to discuss the following day's events.

It was Friday afternoon, and the traffic on the roadway trying to get home for the weekend was stifling. When they pulled up across the street from the bank in the parking lot of the SeaTac Mall, Johnny quickly applied makeup to his face. He added a paste-on black beard and mustache, a blond wig, and finished off his disguise with a pair of thick-rimmed black sunglasses. After his experience at the bank in Montana, Johnny was anxious to see how well the disguises worked here. Frank pulled out of the lot, across the heavy traffic onto S. 320th Street and into the bank parking lot. He dropped Johnny off at the corner of the bank building and then headed off for the rendezvous point they established earlier.

Once Johnny exited the car he realized he was in a vulnerable position. He walked to the north side of the bank and peered in the windows. Just then he saw a van pull up in front of the bank. He approached the driver of the van and ordered him out of the van. When the driver began to argue with him, Johnny pulled a gun from his waistband and forced the driver out from behind the wheel. While this was happening, another customer entering the bank witnessed the events. She ran into the bank and told the security guard that she thought the bank was going to be held up. The security guard then proceeded to go outside where he confronted Johnny at the van. Hearing the security guard's question from behind him, Johnny grabbed the driver of the van by the shirt and spun him around so that he was between him and the guard. By the time the guard saw the gun in Johnny's hand, it was too late. After relieving the driver of the keys to his van, Johnny ordered both men back into the bank. As they entered the bank Johnny ordered everyone in the bank over to the tellers' windows and down on the floor. Then he gave the tellers a green plastic bag and ordered them to fill it up. As he pulled the plastic bag from the brown paper sack that he had carried into the bank, a nylon stocking fell to the floor. When the tellers filled the bag with the money from their cages, Johnny was ready to go. He didn't want anyone following him out of the bank when he left. So, as a deterrent, he decided to give everyone a reason not to. He pulled the security guard up from the floor and preceded to pistol whip him to within an inch of his life. When he finished with the beating, the guard fell to the floor like a limp rag doll. Before leaving, he threatened to repeat the beating to anyone that followed him.

Johnny bolted out the front door, past incoming customers, to the van parked outside. When he reached the van he threw the money in the open driver's side window and got in. At this point, several witnesses stated that they heard a muffled explosion and then a few seconds later saw billowy pink smoke pouring out the windows of the van. What he had forgotten about was the exploding dye packs many banks now had in place. These packs consisted of small explosives, a timer and red dye wrapped in what looked to be a stack of tens or twenties. All the tellers had them in their cash drawers and were instructed to give the packet to a robber when the situation permitted. The purpose of this was twofold. First, the explosion tended to disorient and confuse the suspect. Second, the coating of the money with indelible red dye deprived the suspect of the use of the money by rendered the money useless for exchange either in a store or another bank.

Immediately, Johnny jumped from the van still holding the smoking green plastic bag in one hand. As he got out of the van, he dumped the money from the bag onto the pavement and quickly grabbed what money he felt he could salvage. Then he ran around the side of the bank to the drive-in window where he opened the passenger door of a little gold sports car waiting in line and ordered the driver to drive out of the lot.

Chapter 40

Bob and Andy just finished testifying in a conspiracy trial involving the owner of an insurance agency they arrested while conducting a sting operation in their plainclothes unit of their former precinct. They had just returned to the bullpen from the third-floor courtroom when they received news of the robbery at the People's Bank in Federal Way. Normally they would not be assigned a case in this area but, as luck would have it, the two detectives that normally covered the area swapped some time with them. Today was their day to cover that area. So, although this was an FBI investigation, they were instructed to assist the feds because of the rash of bank robberies that had occurred in the county the last few months.

When they left downtown and got on Interstate 5 both men sighed in disgust as they hit the bumper-to-bumper traffic that awaited them on a Friday afternoon. It was almost two hours before they finally pulled up in front of the bank.

Chapter 41

The gold sports car left the bank parking lot south bound on 23rd Avenue South and drove into the adjoining park-n-ride lot. The car drove through the lot and then down to the medical center at S. 324th Street, across from the shopping mall. From there it traveled south, turning onto 16th Avenue South. Johnny asked the driver if he knew where the Edgewood area was. He was not familiar with the area so Johnny directed him. They drove through the countryside and finally wound up in the Trout Lake area of south King County. Johnny spotted what he believed to be a vacant home and ordered the driver to pull into the driveway. He took him out at gunpoint and walked to the front door. When there was no answer he kicked in the front door and forced him inside. Once inside, Johnny tied him up, stole thirty-five dollars from his wallet and then headed out the door for the sports car. As if he had an after thought, Johnny turned back before he reached the doorway and smashed the butt of his gun across the forehead of his helpless hostage. Then he bounded out the door and fled in the car. After a few minutes, the driver, hurting but conscious, was able to free himself from the ropes. He walked to a nearby neighborhood home where he called the police and an ambulance.

Johnny drove the sports car to the meeting place he and Frank had agreed upon prior to the robbery. When he finally arrived, Frank was showing signs of being just a little bit worried.

"Where the hell have you been?" he chided. "They've already announced the robbery on the radio and the cops are swarming all over. I was gettin' worried that you didn't make it."

"Some unexpected problems came up at the bank," Johnny said as he got out of the sports car and into the Ford, leaving his disguise behind.

After Johnny emptied the contents of his pockets onto the front seat, Frank realized what must have happened with the money from the bank and rolled his eyes in disbelief.

"Are you fuckin' kiddin' me? We took a risk that big for this kind of cash?"

Of the $50,000 taken from the tellers and vault that afternoon, only about $3,000 was salvageable. He had made a critical error this afternoon and he knew it. How could he have forgotten the dye packs?

"Be thankful we got any at all," Johnny continued as he wiped the makeup from his face. "Now let's get the hell out of here and I'll explain what happened on the way back."

Chapter 42

By the time the two detectives arrived at the bank it was early evening and the only ones remaining were the evidence technicians and the bank manager.

"Well, I see that we're just in time to take out the garbage," Andy mused.

Before they were able to get out of the car, they received a call from the police dispatch center to respond to an address in the Trout Lake area where a witness to the bank robbery was waiting to speak with them. The detectives thought it was rather strange that a witness would go all the way home and wait over two hours before they called, but stranger things happened in this business. So without exiting their car, they headed for the Trout Lake address. But before they could exit the parking lot, an evidence technician processing evidence inside the bank came out and caught their attention.

"I've got something here I think you both might want to look at," he said holding up the stocking in his right hand.

"Really now," Andy chuckled. "I don't think we want to know about your personal life."

"Very funny, asshole. This was found on the floor behind the teller's cage."

"Did you do a personal leg check to see if it belongs to one of the tellers?"

"No, but I'm sure you'd like to. There was this blonde," he started, then thought better of it before continuing. "Besides, I checked. They were all wearing panty hose, not stockings. According to one of the tellers the suspect dropped this out of a bag he had them fill with cash."

"Interesting," said Bob as he looked intently at a set of initials embroidered in gold metallic thread at the top of the stocking. "G.L. Where have I seen this before?"

"Seen what before? The stocking?" said Andy. "Are you holding something back from your partner, Bobby my boy?"

"No, you pervert, not the stocking, the initials." He knew they meant something. *Where had he seen them before?*

When they reached the Trout Lake address, it became obvious they had more than just an eyewitness to the robbery. The driver, Michael Ferris, along with the two residents of the small rustic cottage, met both detectives on the front porch. Ferris was holding a bag of ice on the top of his head. He explained to Bob and Andy what happened and gave them a detailed description of the man in the cake makeup and wig. Bob radioed back to the dispatcher to advise them of their situation and request a police artist. Within a few minutes, dispatch responded. They advised him that the FBI had arranged for their artist to meet them downtown. Ferris refused to accept any additional medical treatment, and the two detectives transported him from the cottage back to the FBI office where he provided a description of the suspect to the FBI artist. Those sketches, along with several pictures from the surveillance cameras at the bank, were released the next day to the news media.

After Bob and Andy delivered Mike Ferris downtown to the Federal Building, they returned to their office and gathered a few things they had left behind.

"You know," Bob said, " I've got a bad feeling about this robbery, Andy. I don't know what it is, but all my instincts are telling me that something else is going to happen or has happened before and it involves these same people."

"What do you mean? You think these guys are doing other jobs in the area?"

"You remember me telling you after that shooting at the Chinese restaurant that I've been collecting teletypes from other departments around the Puget Sound area that seem to be related, but really don't have any links...yet? Well, it's just a wild hunch, but I think I've got a connection."

Chapter 43

At 3:30 in the afternoon, one week after the People' Bank in Federal Way was robbed, a blue Ford LTD parked in the Sears parking lot in the city of Redmond. Two males made their way from the car into the store. Johnny had considered the bank job a total failure. The few thousand they salvaged didn't last long with the type of drugs they were buying. Now it was necessary to make additional plans. Johnny always took precautions not to be seen at too many jobs with the same accomplices. Even though Frank was really not with him during the bank job, he felt it necessary to have another person today. This afternoon he chose Jim Green, a Native American he met while serving time in the Washington State Penitentiary in Walla Walla, Washington. Green, a member of one of the local tribes, lived in the north Seattle area and had never been involved in any criminal activity this far east of the city. He was a big man in stature and weighed about 225 pounds, with long black flowing hair and a slight limp. In his younger years he had made a name for himself as a top-notch running back for Roosevelt High School in Seattle. He was rewarded with an all-expenses-paid scholarship at the University of Washington, but after an injury to his knee in his freshman year, he turned to alcohol and drugs to hide his disappointment. Eventually he quit school and was never able to recover from his addiction to either substance. He became a drifter and street person whom the Seattle police became intimately acquainted with on a number of occasions over the years. One of those occasions had led him to the state penitentiary and his eventual relationship with Hardy. Two days prior to their trip to Redmond, he was contacted by Hardy who told him he was looking for someone the police on the east side of Lake Washington were not acquainted with. It didn't take Green very long to agree to help Hardy, especially when he heard there was money to be made.

Once the two men entered the store, they headed straight for the hardware and tool section to make their selection. As they walked down the center aisle of the store, the plainclothes store security person got a bad feeling about both of them. He watched them from a distance as the taller and thinner of the two men placed padlocks and other small tools into the pockets of his parka. While that was going on the other man, the Indian, grabbed half dozen rolls of duct tape and both men headed for the exit.

Without thinking too much about calling for assistance the security guard followed the two men out of the exit door and into the parking lot. He caught up with both men about halfway across the parking lot and called for them to stop. He was totally unprepared for what happened next. Both men stopped dead in their tracks and turned toward him as he approached. When he confronted the men about the locks, Johnny reached into his jacket pocket, pulled out a .38-caliber revolver and put it to his head. Without a word, Green grabbed the security officer's arm and led him to the Ford, parked about three stalls away. He opened the rear door and, without warning, Johnny brought the butt of the revolver down on the security man's head and he collapsed in a heap outside the car.

"What the hell did you do that for?" Jim snarled at Johnny.

"No fuckin' reason," he said. "Just help me put him in the car."

"Are you crazy? What do we want with a security guard?

"I don't know. Maybe we'll kill him. Now help me put him in the car."

Chapter 44

Three hours passed before anyone noticed that the security officer was missing. When the first call went out to police, the evening rush had just begun to snarl traffic around the store. By the time the police officer reached Sears it had been three and a half hours since the abduction. The first officer on the scene interviewed several employees who had seen the security officer earlier in the day, but could not give any information that could be useful.

As luck would have it, an employee who had left work earlier in the day, returned to the store to pick up a package that she had left behind. When she saw the patrol car outside the store and the officer taking a report inside, she questioned another employee regarding the officer's presence. When she was told why he was there, she immediately ran over to the officer. She had been with the security officer earlier that day when he had stopped in her department while observing two men he suspected were shoplifting. While they talked he observed them take locks, tools and tape, and leave the store. The security person left the store following both men. She hadn't seen him after that, and she assumed that he had either recovered the property or arrested the two men. The officer took the description of both men, added it to the report and left the store.

At 9:30 p.m. that evening, almost six hours after the abduction, a blue Ford LTD pulled up to a remote country intersection in north King County. The rear passenger door flew open and the unconscious body of the security officer spilled out onto the pavement. His hands and feet bound in duct tape, he had been severely pistol-whipped but was still alive. A passing motorist found him, cut off the tape, placed him in his car and drove him to the closest fire station in the city of Duvall. The firefighters at the station immediately called the police and then transported the security guard to the hospital.

When the call came out for the county officer to respond to the situation, he had no knowledge of the abduction in Redmond earlier that day. He proceeded to the hospital unaware of what the actual situation was. When he arrived and spoke to the emergency room personnel, he realized the seriousness of the injuries to the victim and decided to contact his supervisor and have him make a decision on whether to call out Major Crimes detectives. He related the details to his supervisor who then made the decision to call in Major Crimes detectives.

When Andy got the call at home that evening, it couldn't have come at a more inopportune time. He had just settled into the lush leather couch in his living room with the redhead from upstairs. With phone in hand, he looked down on her bare breasts and her willing smile, shook his head and dialed Bob's pager number.

The theater was an enormous building containing twelve separate theaters along with a game room, three refreshment counters and a souvenir stand where you could purchase the latest promotional items related to the movies now playing. When the pager vibrated on Bob's belt, he had just sat down with his wife and kids to see a movie he had promised to take them to weeks before. As soon as he read the number he knew who it was. He looked over at his wife and whispered in her ear, "I'll be right back." He didn't think he would have any use for a cell phone that evening so he had left it at home. He got up, left the theater and walked to the phone booth at the front of the building. He dialed Andy's number and waited for two rings before the phone was answered.

"Hey, Bob. We just got the call to an assault. The victim's at Harborview and he's not in great shape. Where are you?"

"I'm in the theater at Alderwood Mall. I've got the wife and kids with me. Can you pick me up? That way my wife can take the kids home in our car."

"Sure thing. I can be there in about fifteen or twenty minutes."

"What lousy timing. It's the first time in months I've been able to get out with everyone."

"You think you've had bad timing, you should be in my shorts."

Bob heard a moaning noise in the background and could just imagine what that meant. "How long did you say it would take you to get here?"

"I'll see you in about twenty minutes."

Andy hung up and Bob returned to the theater to break the news to his wife. She seemed to take the news in stride. She had been a police wife for so long that nothing surprised her. He kissed her good-bye, said, "Don't wait up," kissed and hugged both girls and then headed out to the front of the theater to wait for Andy.

Andy arrived right on time. Bob hopped into the passenger side of the unmarked car and they sped off toward Interstate 5 southbound into Seattle. On the way downtown, Andy filled Bob in on the particulars of the assault. A passing motorist on a country road had found the victim in Duvall. His hands and feet were duct-taped and he had been pistol-whipped severely. The doctors in the ER didn't know if he would make it. The victim had no ID. He was dressed in jeans, a blue shirt and tennis shoes and in a brief moment of consciousness mumbled the word Sears.

Bob picked up the radio and asked the dispatcher to contact the Sears downtown and in several malls in the area to see if anything out of the ordinary had occurred in any of them today. After about five minutes the dispatcher came back on and asked him to switch over to the TAC frequency. (The TAC frequency was used when officers or the dispatcher wanted to transmit sensitive information over a semi-secure frequency. It was utilized mostly to prevent news media and those people who monitored police frequencies from gaining information that would allow them to follow and hound officers on important or sensitive calls.) Once he switched his radio over, the dispatcher related to him the details of the abduction that occurred at the Sears in Redmond earlier that day. Bob told the dispatcher to contact Detective Rick Reed of the Redmond police and let him know what they were responding to.

"Get a number where we can contact him and I'll get it from you on a landline once we get to the hospital."

"Copy. I'll call right away."

When they reached the hospital, Andy parked the car in the police parking slot outside the emergency room. Both men headed in, went directly to the desk and identified themselves. The nurse, who anticipated the arrival of the police, ushered them back to see the doctor. Dr. Rani Shankar met the detectives outside the victim's room. With clipboard in hand, he proceeded to explain to both of them what type of injuries the victim had incurred.

"What do you expect him to do, Doc?" Andy asked.

"The patient is currently in a coma. All his vital signs are on the verge of disappearing. We will not know about his chances for recovery until...," he paused to rephrase his response. "We honestly don't know if he will recover at all."

Bob walked back over to the admitting desk picked up the phone and dialed the number that dispatch had given him for Rick Reed.

"Hey, Rick. It's Bob."

"Bob, what do you have?"

Bob explained what he knew about the victim and what the possibility of recovery, or lack thereof, was. In return Butch relayed the information about the abduction to Bob.

"I'll keep you posted if anything happens here tonight," said Bob. "If you don't hear from me tonight, I'll call you in the morning and we'll get together."

"Thanks. I'll talk to you soon."

Bob walked back to where Andy and Dr. Shankar were discussing the attributes of some of the more, shall we say, endowed nurses. Shankar, with a smirk, turned to Bob and in his Indian accent said, "You know if I were you, I'd keep a very good eye on this one. You need to find him some help real soon."

"Trust me, Doc, I know and I'm looking."

The doctor turned and shuffled on to the next room to check its occupant, all the while shaking his head and smiling.

"Why does everyone think I need help?" Andy pleaded. "Don't you like women too? Huh?"

"Just as much as the next guy, Andy, but—" Before Bob could finish, a commotion erupted in the ER. Nurses and doctors scrambled past them to get into the room now occupied by the victim of their assault. The only sound that either man heard over the noise was the drone of the heart monitor.

"Shit!" Bob muttered, "We didn't want a statement, anyway?"

Chapter 45

The next morning, as Bob and Andy entered the courthouse, they went through their morning ritual of a cup of coffee from the little sandwich/coffee shop located on the main floor. From there they headed off to the bullpen (the detectives' offices) to continue their day. When they were buzzed through the secured door that led into their office, Bob headed straight for his desk, while Andy made a detour to the receptionist's desk to make a date for the weekend.

Bob pulled open the bottom drawer of his desk and opened a file he kept stashed beneath some old criminology textbooks. He removed the teletypes that he saved from the last couple of months and began to diligently scan their contents. One was a rather comical daytime robbery in Montana, where the suspects used makeup and wigs and somehow managed to disable the responding officer's patrol cars by jamming toothpicks into the car locks. About halfway through the pile, he found what he was looking for. He picked up his phone and dialed a number.

"Good morning, Gig Harbor Police"

"May I speak with Detective Sorter, please?"

"One moment while I see if he's in."

"Detective Sorter."

"Detective, this is Bob DeNucci, King County Major Crimes. How's it going?"

"Depends on why you're calling. What can I do for you?"

"You had a burglary about a month or so ago at a residence just outside of town. Last name was Larson."

"Larson? Oh yeah, Larson. Door in the back of the garage was kicked in and then they kicked their way into the house through an entry door in the garage. Two guys were picked up just north of Olympia shortly after with a gun stolen from the burglary."

"What happened to the two guys?"

"Typical liberal-ass judge. Let 'um both go on their own recognizance. As I could have told him, neither one showed up for their first hearing. God knows where they are right now."

"Well, maybe somebody besides God knows where they are."

"What does that mean?"

"Tell me, on your teletype you listed the victim as G. Larson. Does G. Larson happen to be a woman?"

"Sure is. A cute little divorcee."

"She have any clothing taken during the burglary?"

"Now that you mention it, she had quite a lot of clothing taken."

"What about stockings? She list any of those as taken?"

Pulling out the report Sorter checked the missing items. "Well yeah, she did. What about her stockings?"

"She have any identifiable markings on her stockings?"

"Nothing marked on the report."

"Will you do me a favor? Will you give her a quick call and see if she did, then give me a call back?"

"Now you've really got me curious. What's going on?"

"I don't want to jump the gun here. I might just be barking up the wrong tree. Ask her first, and then call me."

"I'll call you right back."

Bob hung up the phone confidant he had his link. But he held off telling Andy about it until he received a call back from Sorter.

If this was the same group of people, what else were they involved in? And why are they branching out to do robberies? He thought for a moment. Maybe they're not branching out. Maybe they've been doing them all along. Maybe he had better widen his search for what these guys are involved in. A lot of maybes. He grabbed his cup and walked up to the front office to retrieve his partner.

When he walked into the reception area, he noticed Andy on his normal morning perch atop the front counter, with his briefcase and gun on the floor, strategically positioned to view the long beautiful legs of the receptionist. He had gotten an extra bonus this morning because she was wearing and exceptionally low-cut dress that perfectly defined her more than ample cleavage. Bob walked over to the counter and took Andy by the arm.

"Come on, partner, if she hasn't said yes by now it's time to give up."

"Not said yes! Are you kidding? Andy continued. "See you on Saturday at seven."

The receptionist blew Andy a kiss as Bob dragged him off the counter and back to the bullpen.

"You know some day you're gonna bite off much more than you can chew."

"Yeah, I know. Ain't that great!"

They had just gotten back to their desks when Bob's phone rang.

"DeNucci."

"Bob, this is Sorter. I just spoke to the victim. It's the strangest thing but she told me that she has a habit of marking all of her clothing."

"Let me guess. Embroidered gold metallic thread with the letters G.L. on everything"

"You got it. Now what's up?"

Bob filled Sorter in on the bank robbery and the stocking, and then explained his theory to him.

"I think these guys, whoever they are, are involved in a lot more then we realize or know about. Will you fax me over a copy of your report with the names of the suspects?"

"Yeah, sure. I'll also send you the arrest report on the two suspects outside of Olympia. You ought to call the officer that arrested them and see if he can give you anything additional."

Bob thanked Sorter for the information and hung up.

"I didn't hear much, but I heard enough to put two and two together. What do you think these guys are involved in?"

"I don't know yet, Andy, but I think we'd better find out before they hit again."

Before the end of the day, Bob and Andy had contacted six other police agencies, from Seattle south to Olympia, who had experienced a rash of burglaries and robberies that could be tied to the group they were now looking for. They asked that each agency forward them copies of their reports, which they would add to their own on-going investigation.

Chapter 46

It was a bright Northwest spring afternoon, something that doesn't occur very often, when a gold Mercury Cougar pulled slowly into the parking lot in downtown Redmond. Flowers were hanging from the light posts as was a custom in many Northwest towns and trees were just beginning to awaken from their winter naps. After parking on the north side of the lot, a male occupant slid out of the passenger side and cautiously walked across the lot, deliberately looking for any signs of trouble. As he entered the boutique, located in the center of the strip mall, the clerk quickly noticed something odd about this person. The person that entered the store appeared, by the manner in which he was dressed, to be a male, about 5'3," long dark hair pulled back into a pony tail, wearing a baseball cap, jeans and heavy sweatshirt and sporting a dark mustache. At first the clerk thought that this was a joke. It was obvious from the protruding breasts that this was a woman disguised as a man. Probably a hoax of some kind, she thought, put on by some of her friends.

But the situation quickly changed. She observed this person grab two coats, some jeans, several hats and scarves and bolt through the front door of the store. It took her a second or two to realize what had just occurred. Then she bolted out the door in pursuit of the thief. Unfortunately, her delay of a few seconds was just enough time for the suspect to jump into the front seat of the gold Ford as it sped past the store and the neighboring gun store and out onto the main road.

The next afternoon, about five p.m., Johnny parked a green AMC Ambassador, stolen from a Redmond driveway only an hour and a half before, in a parking space outside of Sportees gun store. Two individuals exited the car and walked into the gun store. No one took any notice that both individuals were wearing disguises which included fake mustaches, wigs and pancake makeup.

The taller of the two went directly to the back of the store where he approached an employee. The shorter of the two waited inside the front door. As the taller individual, later identified as Hardy, approached the employee he withdrew a small .25-caliber automatic from his jeans. He placed the snub-nose into the employee's ribs and ordered him into the back room. A customer overheard the commotion in the rear and saw what was happening. As he tried to leave the store to try and get help, Nora pulled a .38-caliber snub-nosed revolver from her coat pocket and confronted him. Fumbling with the gun as she pulled it from her pocket, she did not realize she had dropped something on the floor. Nora led him to the back where Johnny had the employee and then returned to the front of the store. As she got back to the front door, another customer entered. Once again, she repeated the trek to the back of the store with the customer, but this time remained with Johnny, who was in the process of chaining and taping the employees and customers with the materials he had stolen from the Sears store in Redmond. As Johnny taped up the last customer, Nora reached down, took the customer's wallet from his back pocket and removed $78 from the billfold. When she had finished, she joined Johnny at the store counter and helped him remove twenty-five assorted handguns from the glass gun cases. When neither could handle another gun, they made a beeline for the front door. But before they could get to the door, Sherry Green, a lovely young blonde in her late twenties taking a break from her job at a local retailer, opened the front door and entered.

Investigators who interviewed the witnesses later that afternoon pieced together what happened next. It seems when Green entered Sportees, she immediately felt something was wrong. But instead of following her instincts and leaving the store, she proceeded toward the front counter. There in the center of the aisle, halfway between the gun counter and the front door, Nora collided, head-first, with Sherry Green. At the moment of impact, Nora was gripping the snub-nose revolver in her right hand while her left hand and arm were full of stolen weapons. As the two women collided, the impact caused Nora to squeeze off a round that inadvertently struck the audible alarm located over the front door of the store. As the bell rang wildly, Johnny, who was less than two steps behind Nora, ran into both women, knocking them to the floor. In doing so, Nora spilled the stolen guns across the aisle. As quickly as she had been knocked down, Sherry, now sensing the danger she was in, was up on her feet and headed for the door. In the ensuing panic, Johnny, who was carrying a pillowcase full of stolen weapons, lifted Nora by the back of the pants as she was frantically grabbing for the spilled weapons. When she got to her feet, Johnny had already passed her and was chasing Green out the front door.

When Sherry Green pulled open the front door of Sportees, she instinctively ran for her parked car. But before she could step off the curb in front of the store, Hardy caught up with her knocked her to the ground and loomed over her. Luckily for Green, the sound of the audible alarm from the gun store now began to draw a crowd of gawking onlookers from the surrounding shops. Hardy, realizing the predicament he was in, quickly composed himself, turned and ran for the parked AMC. Stunned and bleeding from the left knee through her ripped jeans, Green watched as the shorter of the two suspects bolted out the front door with an arm full of guns and joined the other suspect at the green AMC where they got into the car and quickly drove from the parking lot.

As every cop knows, the first officer on the scene of a major crime will have a substantial influence on the outcome of the investigation because of what he or she does or doesn't do. The first officer to respond to Sportees was a seasoned cop with over ten years of street experience. What he did that afternoon to secure the scene and protect the physical evidence upon his arrival turned out to be one of the breaks investigators would look back on and proclaim to be a key factor in identifying and capturing the suspects.

Detective Rick Reed of the Redmond Police Department was contacted and informed of the gun store robbery. When he was advised of the suspects' M.O. and the manner in which the victims had been bound, he responded to the scene immediately. After he arrived, he did a cursory search of the crime scene, and then placed a call to Bob DeNucci downtown.

Chapter 47

Bob was seated at his desk, contemplating and studying the teletypes he had gathered from around the area, when he received the call from Reed.

"Hey, Rick, how the hell are ya?"

"Bob, you're not going to believe this, but our buddies with the chain and tape from the Sears store showed up in downtown Redmond this afternoon."

"No shit. What happened?"

"They hit a little gun shop on the eastside of town at Bear Creek Village. Tied up the owner and some customers with tape, locks and chains that we've already determined came from the Sears kidnaping-homicide."

"Any luck on an ID?"

"Not yet, but I thought you might like to come on over and take a look at the scene. Maybe even talk to some to the witnesses."

"Hell, yes. It'll take us about a half hour to get there. See you then."

When Bob hung up the phone, Andy knew from the expression on his face that something had happened. Bob filled him in on the robbery in Redmond then they gathered their things and headed to the county garage to pick up their car and head toward the eastside.

Chapter 48

When they arrived at Bear Creek Village in Redmond, it didn't take them long to pick out the store where the robbery occurred. Sportees was completely surrounded by patrol cars from the Redmond and King County Police, the latter of which were called in as back-up. As the two detectives drove up to the front of the store, an officer on the scene directed them to a parking space. They parked their car and walked to the command post, which was set up outside the store.

"Hey, Rick."

Rick Reed was busy talking to one of the evidence techs and turned as he heard the two men approaching. "Hi, Andy. How's it going, Bob? This has to be our homicide suspects. I just had a Sears' representative verify the packaging that was on the locks. It's their packaging."

"You get any prints?" asked Andy.

"They're in there dusting right now. From what I saw, I think we've got some good ones."

"Can we go in?"

"Sure, follow me."

The three men passed under the yellow crime scene tape and entered the already opened front door of the gun shop. An officer was in the process of gingerly lifting an unloaded .357 Magnum from the aisle where one of the suspects had dropped it on the way out. As the three men slowly walked down the aisle, they scanned the store for any clues that might have been overlooked. They reached the front counter that now consisted of two broken glass cases that the guns were removed from. As another officer went about the business of dusting the counter area, the three detectives stood and looked out the window on the east side of the building contemplating the ramifications of this robbery.

"Now we've really got trouble," Bob said. "Not only do they have the balls to commit this type of crime and others like it in broad daylight, now they have the tools to help them." Worriedly he posed the question, "What can we do to help, Rick?"

"Right now, Bob, I'm not so sure. We could get the word out on the street about these people, but I'm afraid that once the word hit the streets, these guys will go underground."

"Unless we get some kind of break on this, do we have a choice?" Andy asked.

Rick led the men back toward the front door and the command post where the witnesses were located.

"No, I agree with you. We have to take the chance that these guys might split. But I've got a bad feeling that won't happen."

Suddenly, Bob stopped in his tracks and stared down at the floor. There, sticking out from under the open door was a white circular tag, the type of tag you would find on the end of a key chain. Bob picked up the tag and looked at the letters and numbers printed on it.

"Maybe, just maybe, we have that break we need."

Chapter 49

The three men sat at Reed's desk and looked over the small circular item that Bob had picked up from the floor of the gun shop. There on the front of the tag was a post office box number from the Carnation Post Office. Carnation was a tiny farming community, about forty-five minutes northeast of Seattle, in the Snoqualmie River Valley, whose claim to fame was that it was once the home to the famous Carnation Research and Dairy Farms.

"No one at the gun shop laid claim to the tag," said Bob. "I'd say for the time being, and because we have nothing better to go on right now, we don't look a gift horse in the mouth. Let's just assume our perps, for whatever reason, dropped this tag. Let's give the postmaster a call and see what type of information we can get from it."

Ten minutes later, Andy was on the phone with the local postmaster giving him the post office box number and requesting the information they needed. When he hung up, he turned and said, "He'll call back this afternoon with the information. In the meantime, I could use a cup of coffee."

"Yeah, that sounds..." Bob stopped in mid-sentence. "Say, Rick, I've got a hunch. It's just a hunch, but do you think you could swing it so that the slug the perps left in the alarm system goes over to the state lab?"

"The slug? What for?"

"I'd like to get it over to Kelly Egan at Seattle to match it up to a slug from a shooting and robbery that occurred on Greenwood a short time ago."

"You think these guys are responsible for that?" Andy chimed in.

"Just a hunch. But I'd like to have it checked out."

"Let me check with my boss. We'll probably send it to the state lab anyway."

"Good, I'll give Kelly a call and let him know about the slug. He can arrange to have the slug compared to those from his shooting."

Reed decided against coffee, it was bad for his ulcer, so Andy and Bob headed for one of the closest cop coffee shops in the area, Denny's Restaurant. As they downed their second cup of coffee, Andy got a call from the dispatch center asking him to call the postmaster. When he returned from the pay phone he slid into their booth with a smile on his face.

"Pay dirt! The box is rented to a Terry Fox with a Carnation address. Shall we?"

"Most certainly," replied Bob.

They slid out of their booth, paid for the coffee and headed for their car. Bob stopped at the phone booth in the restaurant to make a phone call.

"Detective Egan," the voiced boomed on the other end.

"Hello, you miserable leprechaun," Bob kidded the big man.

"Is that you, you smelly WOP?" He threw the insult right back.

Bob went on to fill Egan in on the slug and the possible connection.

"Thanks, Bob. I'll get right on it and see what happens. You know, you're not half bad for a WOP."

As they approached the house on the West Snoqualmie Valley Road, there was no sign of activity. The white two-story farmhouse with black shutters and a rundown porch was dark and by the looks of the yard no one had been there for quite a while. They gave Rick Reed a call and passed on the information about the house, then decided that tomorrow they would contact the pro-active unit at their old precinct and ask them for some surveillance help.

By that time their shift was just about over, and the two men headed home. It was Bob's week to drive so he dropped Andy off at his apartment first and then headed home. As he drove away, he glanced in his rear view mirror just long enough to see the beautiful redheaded siren bounce out the front door of the apartment complex and greet Andy with a hug.

Chapter 50

Andy and Bob were tied up the entire next day on the fifth floor of the courthouse giving testimony on a drug case. At the conclusion of their testimony, they headed back down to the bullpen area where they picked up their messages for the day and headed up north to the second precinct to contact their old plainclothes unit. Traffic, which was becoming more and more of a problem in the Seattle area, was at a standstill on Interstate 5 as they crawled across the Ship Canal Bridge past the University District. Although both men seemed to be engrossed in an argument regarding the pros and cons of Andy's date for the evening, the lovely redhead at his apartment, they had an uncanny ability to keep one ear tuned to the police frequency on their car radio, now set to the North Precinct area. Just as Andy got into the down and dirty "pros" of his date, that ominous high-pitched tone sounded. They both knew the sound well and immediately stopped their conversation. It was a robbery alert. When the tone stopped the dispatcher continued.

"All North Precinct units, I have a report of an armed robbery of the Jewel Box jewelry store NE 172 and 62 Avenue NE, Kenmore. Suspect description to follow."

"Crap! Wouldn't you know, we're stuck in traffic and this has to happen?"

Andy threw the blue Kojak light on the dashboard of their car while Bob steered toward the shoulder of the freeway.

The dispatcher continued, "All north units, we have a description of suspect one: male, six feet, dark hair in pony tail with blue hat and wearing what the victim describes as heavy pancake makeup. Suspect two, a female, five-foot-six, dark hair tucked under a cowboy hat, also wearing pancake makeup. Both suspects fled in an unknown vehicle, license unknown, from street behind the store." After a pause the broadcast continued. "A witness who observed the two suspects with handguns removing jewelry from the inside counters is reporting this robbery. The witness also reports that the suspects fled up the incline behind the store."

Andy looked over at Bob, who nodded as they both said in unison, "That's got to be our guys."

Andy picked up the car radio and advised the dispatcher and the responding units that they were responding from the freeway. The car slid down the shoulder of I-5 toward the exit ramp on Lake City Way where it exited and responded light and siren to the call.

Chapter 51

Johnny and Nora got up early in the morning and watched the sun rise through the front window of the dilapidated two-story house in north Seattle. Everyone was asleep so they decided to go out. When they left the house the dew was still thick on the windshield and front hood of the blue Ford. Johnny started the car and turned on the windshield wipers to clear their view. While the car warmed up, he reached over and grabbed a little duffel bag off the back seat. He opened the zipper and revealed the contents within to Nora. Besides two of the handguns from the Sportees robbery, the bag contained pancake makeup, wigs, hats and sunglasses.

Several days before they had driven to Kenmore and checked out a small jewelry store located in Kenmore Village. Johnny liked what he saw and decided that this would be their target today. He told her what the plan was, then pulled out of the alley and headed toward the interstate. A short trip south took them to the exit for the Evergreen floating bridge, officially the Governor Albert D. Rosellini Bridge—Evergreen Point, the longest floating bridge in the world at 7,578 feet (2,310 meters). It was a huge four-lane cement structure floating on top of the lake which was one of two bridges that crossed Lake

Washington and linked the downtown Seattle area to its eastern suburbs. Once across the bridge, Johnny pulled off the freeway and stopped for breakfast in the upscale city of Bellevue. When they finished breakfast they drove through Bellevue and the adjoining city of Kirkland, hunting for a vehicle that could be used that day. They found the vehicle around one o'clock in the afternoon parked in a small shopping center located in the north Kirkland area on Juanita Drive. The driver conveniently left the door open and the keys in the car. Nora moved into the driver's seat of the blue Ford as Johnny quickly slid into the front seat of a late-model gold Chrysler. Within a minute both cars were head northbound out of the parking lot toward their destination in Kenmore. About a mile from the jewelry store, Johnny motioned for Nora to pull over and park. Nora parked the Ford, grabbed the duffel bag from the back seat, got out of the car and locked the doors. She handed the duffel bag to Johnny and got in the passenger side of the Chrysler. As Johnny pulled away from the curb, she grabbed the duffel bag and withdrew some of its contents. She applied the makeup, put a hat on over a wig, donned a pair of sunglasses and tucked one of the small-caliber handguns into the waistband of her jeans. Moments later the car came to a halt on a bluff overlooking the rear of the jewelry store. Johnny quickly applied the makeup to his face, donned the other items in the bag and grabbed a pillowcase that he had previously taken from the Ford.

Nora looked over at Johnny and began to worry out loud. "It's almost three in the afternoon and we could run into some problems if we're not careful. You know we're parked on a residential street."

Although Johnny normally took great pains to case any neighborhood they might be working in, this time he had not, leaving the possibility that they could be seen by people in the area. It was about time for the school buses to be dropping off students back into their neighborhoods. The last thing they needed was a group of kids screwing up their job. He realized he had made a major mistake, but he had decided to hit the jewelry store and once he made up his mind he was not inclined to change it. So, when Johnny opened his door and got out; she followed.

They both scrambled down the incline that led from the end of the residential street to the back of the building that held the jewelers, a cleaners, TV repair store and a planned parenthood clinic. Johnny slithered up the side of the building while Nora stayed close behind. When he reached the front corner of the building, he peered around into the front window. There, behind the counter, he spotted the elderly couple that owned the business going about their daily chores. There was no one else in the store so he waved Nora up to his side and then both quickly turned the corner and entered the store.

There was no doubt in the old couple's mind as to what was happening when the two odd-looking people enter the front door. The man rose from his stool behind the counter and headed directly for the phone that lay on the counter about ten feet away. Johnny bounded across the store and was on him before he could lift up the receiver. Nora drew her gun from her jeans and was holding it across the front counter in the face of the woman. They herded the owners into the back room of the store and immediately went about the business of padlocking and taping both of them to two chairs they found there. Once that was accomplished, they emptied the entire jewelry counter into the pillowcase that Johnny was carrying and quickly left the store through the front entrance.

As they exited the store, Nora nearly collided with a customer standing on the sidewalk in front of the store. The startled customer froze as he watched both Johnny and Nora, with guns in hand, go up the incline and disappear from his view on the road above the store.

Cautiously he went into the store, not knowing what to expect. When he found the owners bound in the back of the room he released them and they called the police.

Chapter 52

By the time Bob and Andy arrived at the scene, the area was saturated with police units. Bob contacted the supervisor who was with the owners inside the store while Andy spoke with several witnesses gathered at one of the patrol cars outside.

Bob looked at the chain and lock that was used on the owners of the business. It was an exact duplicate of the one used in the Redmond Sportees robbery. *These guys, whoever they were, were certainly not shy about these day time robberies.* He wondered how much longer till someone was hurt or killed again. They couldn't let that happen, yet, at this point they were powerless to prevent it. Bob's train of thought was interrupted by a nudge from Andy.

"Hey, you want to talk to any of the witnesses?"

"Yeah, is there anyone here from the street behind the jewelers?"

"No, not that I'm aware of. Just the guy who saw the two when they bumped into him coming out of the store and a couple that witnessed our perps run from the store."

"Why don't you finish up talking to them and I'll go knock on some doors up on the hill behind the building and see what I can scope out."

Bob headed up the hill to the residential street behind the small shopping center. He knocked on the first door and was greeted by a young woman in her thirties carrying a baby wrapped in a blue blanket. He identified himself and produced a badge and identification card from a black leather wallet in his rear pocket.

"Oh, you mean those strange people that were parked across the street?"

"What strange people would you be talking about?"

"A man and a woman pulled up in a gold car, I'm not real good with cars, and I don't know what it was. Anyway, they pulled up and parked. I just put the baby down for a nap when I walked out to the living room and noticed the gold car parked across the street. It was really odd.'

"What was odd?"

"Well, the man who was driving, had curly light brown hair. I watched him as he reached into some kind of bag or something in the front seat and he pulled out a wig and placed it on his head. Then he put a hat and sunglasses on and got out of the car with the woman who was in the car with him."

"Did you see where they went?"

"Yes, they walked to the end of the street and then went down toward the shopping center."

"Didn't that seem awfully strange to you?"

"Well, yes it did. But so many people park up here and then go down to the shopping center that even these weirdos didn't faze me."

"Was there anything else you could tell me about these two or their car? Did you get a plate number? Did the car have any unusual characteristics?"

"No, I'm, sorry," she said, embarrassed for not realizing the obvious. "Nothing that I took any notice of."

Bob couldn't get any other information from the woman so he wrapped up the interview and headed down the block toward the other homes. After knocking on about six or seven doors and coming up empty-handed, Bob decided to call it quits. As he turned to leave the last house a little boy about ten years old approached him.

"Are you a policeman?" he quizzed.

"Yes, son, I am."

"Are you here because of the robbery?"

"Yes, I am."

"Were those two people in the gold Chrysler the bad guys?"

Bob stopped walking. "What two people?" he quizzed the little boy

"You know. The ones with the guns."

"Tell me about them, son," he said hopefully. "Did you get a look at them?"

"Sure. But they didn't see me. I was hiding on the side of the house. They came up from the shopping center and I saw them take off their wigs and hats. Then they got in the car and wiped off their make up."

"You said they had guns. Did you actually see the guns?"

"You bet. The girl had a small handgun and the guy had an automatic like the toy one my dad bought me for my birthday."

"What did they look like?"

"The girl was like Chinese I think. She had long dark braids. The guy was white. He had curly hair and was tall."

"What about the car?"

"Oh that's easy. I love cars. I even wrote down the license plate." He pulled from his pocket a crumpled piece of paper that looked like it had just been ripped from the corner of a small notebook. On the paper, written in pencil, were the letters CBA and numbers 234.

Bob got the boy's name and address and then headed back toward the store and his partner. He asked Andy for the portable he was carrying and then called the license plate number the boy had given him into dispatch. Moments later he received the response that the car, a gold 1978 Chrysler had just been reported stolen from a shopping center just south of

Kenmore. He asked the dispatcher to broadcast the vehicle as a possible suspect vehicle in the armed robbery and alert the officers on duty that if found, more than likely the car had been ditched in the area and to handle it for prints and other evidence.

Andy and Bob returned to their car, where they both filled each other in on what they had found out. Then Andy got on the radio and requested that the pro-active unit on duty contact them at the precinct a few blocks away.

Upon their arrival at their old precinct, they parked in the front parking lot and went in through the front door. Anne, ever so lovely in her short kilt-type skirt wrapped around her waist, greeted them.

"Annnnndyyyy!" she whined. "Don't you start spreading any unsubstantiated rumors!" (Referring to their recent visit to Major Gregory's house.)

"Me, rumors…no way. Now, on the other hand…"

"Down, boy," Bob said lunging to catch the back of Andy's collar as he leaned over the front counter of the precinct to get a closer look at Anne's velvety thighs. "You've got your hands full with that redhead…remember?"

"No harm in looking, is there?" Andy whimpered with a smile as Bob pulled him back across the counter.

"Don't worry, Anne, your secret's safe with us." Then giving Andy that fatherly look, he said, "I'll make sure of that." Bob was no fool, he knew that Anne was someone he wanted on his side, not as an enemy, should the time ever come that he needed inside information. He just needed to remind Andy about the facts of life in the police department.

Andy straightened up his sports coat and both men passed through the "employees only" door that led to the offices at the back of the precinct. They walked down a small corridor past the captain and lieutenant's office and then out into an open area used by the precinct's burglary and larceny detectives. Bob stopped at one of the empty desks and grabbed a pad of paper lying on it before they entered the office. No one was there yet, so while Andy made himself comfortable, Bob walked to the report room on the other side of the precinct and got them both a cup of black coffee. By the time he returned to the office, Andy was shootin' the shit with Hal Grogen and Dave Green, two of the unit's best.

Hal was the former chief of police of a small rural police department in Island County, Washington. He came to the department about the same time as Bob and was working toward a promotion into the narcotics unit ever since. Dave Green, on the other hand, had been in the patrol division of the department close to fifteen years, and had just recently been transferred into the pro-active unit. He was happy to be where he was and had no intentions of going any further. That is, unless he passed the sergeant's test next month.

Bob and Andy relayed the information to both officers regarding the suspected safe house in the Carnation area. Bob wrote the address on the pad tore off the top sheet of paper and handed it to Hal.

"If you guys would do us a favor and keep an eye on this place, we'd appreciate it."

"How often do you want us check it?" asked Hal.

"And what do you want us to do if we find somebody there?" Dave questioned

"I'd say at least once a shift. Also, if anything major goes down in the area, maybe you could mosey over and check out what type of activity you have. If you do find someone there, get hold of Andy or me. If we're not working, have them page us or call us at home. We're interested in whoever shows up there."

"You've got it. If someone's hanging around there, we'll find 'um."

"And be careful. These guys now have the fire power to make life...or death miserable."

"We'll be more careful than you guys."

"What do you mean?" asked Andy.

"I mean, drinking that rot-gut crap from the back, you've got a lot more chance of dying from an untimely death than we ever will," Dave said with a laugh. "Obviously being big-shot detectives has warped your brain. Let's go and get some good stuff. We'll meet you at Denny's in Kenmore."

Chapter 53

DeNucci was at his desk downtown in the bullpen when he received the phone call from Rick Reed of the Redmond Police Department. Reed just received information from an informant that Tommy Fox and his girlfriend were holed up at a residence at N. 80th and Aurora Avenue N. When he hung up, DeNucci called the pro-active unit at the North Precinct. He arranged to have four pro-active officers assigned to him for the evening. (While on the phone, DeNucci scribbled a note to himself to remember to pick up some mug shots of individuals suspected to be Fox and his girlfriend.) As of yet, no one really knew exactly who they were or what they looked like since no booking photos were taken after the burglary arrest around Olympia. When he got off the phone he searched the bullpen for his partner. Knowing just where to look, he walked over to Anderson's desk, grabbed his holster and gun from the desk drawer and then went directly to the front office, where he found Anderson flirting with the receptionist.

"Come on, we've got a date with a scum bag," he whispered as he grabbed Anderson by the arm and led him out the door.

"Where the hell are we going?" was his first response, then, "Is it really better than where I was?"

"No, I don't suppose it is, but we're going anyway."

Before they left the building, they stopped in the records department and quickly picked up the mug shots that DeNucci had just requested. Bob grabbed the photos from the clerk and tossed them into his briefcase.

By the time they reached the county garage, Bob had filled Andy in on what was going on. They found their brown, standard police-issue Dodge Diplomat and headed up James Street toward northbound Interstate 5. When they reached the ramp at 80th, they exited and headed eastbound toward Green Lake where they planned to meet the other officers.

It was about three o'clock when they pulled into the lot at Green Lake. The weather was unusually warm for this time of year. They tried to find shade in the parking lot, but the sun continued to blare down on the top of the Diplomat through the sparsely leafed trees, making them both feel as though they were sitting in an oven. It was still too cool for the air conditioning so they removed their jackets and ties, rolled up their sleeves and waited. About twenty-five minutes later, the pro-active officers arrived at their location. While they sat talking to the other officers, a silver station wagon pulled into the lot sixty-nine style alongside DeNucci's side of the car and the lone occupant, unshaven and chewing on the stub of an old cigar, rolled down his window.

"I heard you on the radio, what are you up to now?" growled their supervisor.

Sgt. Don Levi was a twenty-five-year veteran of the police force. He had spent many of those years as a street cop and then sergeant in the Patrol Division of the North Precinct. Known more for his bark than his bite, most of the officers in the precinct knew he had a soft spot for the men who worked under him. He'd been DeNucci's supervisor the first few years he was with the department and was instrumental in his reassignment from the patrol division to the pro active unit when Levi had taken command. He found out soon after his transfer downtown that it was Levi who spoke up for him and Anderson when they were promoted to detective, not Barnett as they had both thought. Both DeNucci and Levi developed a mutual self-respect for each other's capability and had become good friends both on and off duty.

"Hello, boss." Anderson grinned as he leaned over from the passenger side of the vehicle. "We just received information that the perps we've been looking for are shacked up at a house on 80th and Aurora. We got hold of the pro-act unit up north and they're going to help us with the stake-out."

"Yeah, and Redmond is sending a couple of detectives as well, so I think we're covered," Bob joined in.

"Well, I'll be out and about this evening, so if anything comes of this fiasco, get hold of me."

"Sure thing, Sarge. Should we call you at home or over the radio?" Andy chuckled.

Trying to look his most official disapproval look, Levi leaned out the window of his car and growled at Anderson, "None of your fuckin' business, asshole. You know, if it weren't for your partner keepin' your ass out of trouble, you'd still be pickin' up garbage in the ghetto," Levi said, referring to Anderson's previous employment. A huge smile came across Levi's face as he pulled his head back into his car. He spit out his old stub, grabbed a cigar from his shirt pocket, lit it up and blew the first puff of smoke out the opened window. "One of these days, Anderson, your ass is mine," he laughed as he put the wagon in gear and pulled out of the lot.

"Shit, do you think I offend him?" Andy mocked. They both laughed at Levi's threats, but knew in a pinch, you couldn't find a better boss.

Within a few minutes of Levi's departure, detectives from the Redmond Police Department arrived. They all gathered for a few minutes to discuss their plan. Then one by one each car containing two officers exited the parking lot and headed to their designated location.

The turn-of-the-century two-story, wood-frame and brick building sat between a used car lot and a strip mall of local businesses. Because of the time of day and the fact that it was facing into the setting sun, it was impossible to tell whether lights were on in the house or if people were home. The first hint of movement at the residence occurred as the sun began to set in the western sky. An older model blue Ford pulled up in the alleyway next to the house and two females carrying bags of groceries got out and scurried up the back stairs. Because their backs were to them, it was impossible to tell who either one of the women were.

Anderson radioed to one of the other units. "Any of you guys have a better view?"

"Yeah," one of the units answered, "two females, one Indian, and one was either Asian or Indian. She was going too fast for me to get a good look."

"One of them has got to be her," said Andy as he looked over at Bob, "even the car is a match to our suspects."

"I know," said Bob, "but let's wait and see if anyone else is there. I really want the psycho. Let's see if he comes out." Bob picked up the radio and spoke softly, "Let's give it a little more time, guys, and see if the fox comes out of his den." He laughed at his little pun, then put the radio down and waited.

As the sun crept down below the tree line, everyone settled back to take a breather and wait it out. While Andy took a short snooze, Bob watched. He knew that every other pair of officers was doing the same. As 8:30 rolled around, Bob was about to wake up Andy when all of a sudden the back door of the residence burst open and two males ran down the back steps to the car. Before Bob could get to the radio, both men had entered the Ford and it was rolling down the alley. Andy jumped with the first crackle of their radio.

"Did you see them?" the car radio screeched.

"No! Where?" responded another.

"Down the alley," shouted Bob.

"We've got him," yelled one of the pro-active units.

The Ford drove south down the alley behind the row of businesses and turned right, where it had to stop for a red light at the intersection with Aurora Avenue N. Luckily, this gave the pro-active unit enough time to get out from their vantage point and head south on Aurora and intercept the vehicle.

"Everyone else stay put, we've got him in sight." Unfortunately for the two officers, the light in their direction did not change to red. They were forced to go south on Aurora, right past the suspect vehicle while it was stopped and waiting to make a left turn southbound onto Aurora Avenue N. Now the problem was how to slow down without attracting too much attention and let the suspects pass them so they could get into a good position to make a stop. But as usual, Murphy struck again. The two officers, caught in the inside lane of traffic, watched as the suspect's car just barely caught up to them in the outside lane. Just as the car appeared to be pulling even with them, it made a quick right-hand turn and sped off eastbound on a side street, leaving to two officers with nothing more than a quick glimpse of the occupants.

"Shit," Bob mumbled after hearing of their bad luck. "Everyone stay tight, we still have the women in the house. Maybe our luck will change with them. Did they make the two of you?" he asked the two officers still traveling south on Aurora.

"We're not in one of your standards, so no way they made us. Just Murphy rearing his ugly head again."

No sooner had those last words come over the radio when Bob spotted one of the women come out of the house; smoking and walk north up the alley toward 80th and Aurora.

"This one's ours," said Bob as he started up the car and put it in drive.

They waited for just a moment until the female committed herself to Aurora Avenue northbound.

"Let's get her, Andy. I'll drive you far enough down Aurora and drop you off so you can approach from the front. I'll double back, park and come up from behind."

"How come you get all the fun?" Andy said with a smile.

"Not even with yours, brother, not even with yours," said Bob.

The Diplomat raced up the street, far enough ahead of the female so as not cause undue concern on her part. Andy exited the car on about 90th and Aurora and began his trek back, while Bob circled the block and parked behind her. As Andy approached, he sensed a look from the woman that told him maybe they were not as tricky as they thought. As he neared the suspect, he withdrew a pack of cigarettes from his shirt pocket and approached her for a match. Nora hesitated for a split second and then reached into her purse. Living with Johnny all this time had given her instincts she could never have gained on her own. When she pulled her hand from the purse it contained a small caliber handgun which she began to bring up into Andy's face. Andy sensed the danger, but a little too late, and just stood paralyzed.

"Not today, honey!" a firm but soft voice whispered in her left ear as the barrel of a .9mm automatic screwed into her right.

"Now very slowly, 'cause I wouldn't want to hurt you, drop the gun from your hand, back into your purse or I'll blow your brains all over Aurora."

Nora, totally unprepared for what had just occurred, was visibly shaken and quickly dropped the gun back into her purse.

"Grab her purse, Andy!" Bob shouted, shocking Andy out of his trance.

Andy grabbed the purse and then both of them proceeded to pat her down and put her in cuffs.

"One in the bucket," Bob repeated over his portable radio.

They walked Nora back to their car and placed her in the back seat. Before either of them got back in the car, Bob asked, "You OK, partner?"

"Yeah, I'm fine." But obviously still shaken, he continued, "Do you think she would have pulled the trigger?"

"No telling now. Do you want me to ask her?" Bob motioned toward the back seat of the car.

"No, no, I don't think I really want to know."

When they met with the detectives from Redmond, about three blocks west of the house, the first thing Bob did was remove the gun from the purse. He unloaded it and gave it to one of the detectives to see if they could match it to any of the guns stolen from the Sportees robbery. Within minutes it was identified as one of the gun taken from the Sportees robbery.

Well, thought Bob, *maybe our luck is about to change.*

Chapter 54

After the arrest of Nora Chin, a.k.a. Bonnie, a.k.a. Jean, and a.k.a. Francis, Andy contacted Sgt. Levi and told him what they had. While the sergeant responded to the scene, Bob drafted an affidavit for a search warrant for the suspect's house. While the other officers at the scene maintained surveillance on the suspect's house, Bob and Andy drove over to the residence of Seattle District Court Judge "Wild Bill Lewis." Lewis, a strong police advocate on the bench was a favorite magistrate among all the local police departments. Being for warned of the visit by a phone call from the communication center, he was waiting for the officers in a pair of brown slacks and a white terrycloth robe. He invited them into his home and while both officers waited quietly in the parlor area the judge went about reviewing the affidavit. Fifteen minutes later both officers left the Judge's home, search warrant in hand, for the home on 80th and Aurora Avenue N. The search warrant took less than an hour and a half to serve with little or no evidence being secured. Linda, the only person at the residence when the warrant was served, was identified and released, since she could not be tied to any of the robberies being investigated. The evidence that was secured, a few blank pages of driver's license forms from Oregon and some identification in the name of Terry and Bonnie Fox, was packaged, marked and sent to the evidence room downtown with Anderson who was returning to town to pick up something he had left behind...the receptionist.

Had Bob known that the ride home with Sgt. Levi would take a slight detour for him, he might have thought twice about sliding in the passenger side of the silver wagon. As it was, both men left the scene around midnight after the other suspects did not return home. As Levi's car traveled down the entrance ramp of the freeway, both men were taken by surprise as a dark-colored four-door Dodge sped past the wagon on the right shoulder of the entrance ramp. At the very last second, the Dodge veered to the left, sideswiping the passenger side of the sergeant's car. Immediately, Levi turned on his emergency lights and forced the speeding vehicle off to the side of the entrance ramp where both cars came to a stop, parallel to one another. Bob jumped out of the wagon to confront the driver of the Dodge whom he was closest to. The driver, a white male in his mid twenties, rolled down his window, belched and asked DeNucci what the hell he wanted. As the driver became more belligerent, the odor of alcohol from his breath was enough to make DeNucci tipsy, so he asked the driver to step out of his vehicle.

As soon as the driver began to exit the car, Bob knew he had made a bad mistake. No slouch himself, he had to crane his neck to look up to the behemoth that exited the vehicle. A heated conversation between the two men ensued and it was then Bob knew if he didn't do something to get in the first punch, this monster was going to chew him up and spit him out. Levi, hearing the commotion, put down his radio and hurried out of the car carrying his metal Kellite flashlight.

Meanwhile, Bob knew that the inevitable was about to happen, Faking an attempt to leave, he turned halfway around before he stopped in mid stride and spun himself back at the giant. His first blow shattered the big man's nose spraying blood all over Bob. It also startled him long enough for Bob to grab him by the coat and spin him around onto the hood of the Dodge. That didn't last long. With the strength of two men this huge youngster pushed off the car, catching DeNucci off balance, and picked him up like a rag doll in a bear hug. Bob managed to get his left arm free and instinctively grabbed a hand full of the man's hair, yanking it as hard as he could in a backwards motion. That's when he felt the pain to the top of his hand. While he had been waltzing around with the giant, Sgt. Levi had come up behind them and with all his might took a swing at the head of the man with his Kellite. Bob gave out a yell and instinctively released the man's hair. Now he was in real trouble as he felt his chest slowly being squeezed so he couldn't breathe.

Suddenly, as if by magic, the muscular arms around his chest released him and the man slumped to the ground. There, standing where the giant once towered, was Sgt. Levi, Kellite in hand, with a huge grin on his face.

"We'd better get that hand taken care of," he said as he reached out and grabbed Bob by the arm.

Later, at the hospital when the doctor had finished placing the four stitches in the back of his hand, both men laughed about the last event of the evening. But on the trip back home, Bob wondered to himself if this might be the start of another run of bad luck.

When Andy picked Bob up for work the next morning, he had slept less than two hours. He was unshaven, his eyes were the color of a bloody Mary and his hand was bandaged up to his wrist. The only saving grace was he had talked Levi into allowing him to wear jeans and a sweater to work that day instead of the usual shirt, tie and jacket routine.

"What the hell happened to you?"

"Just drive, I'll explain as I come to my senses. First things first, we ran out of coffee this morning and I need a cup...quick."

"Sure thing, partner. Shit, I thought I looked bad yesterday after that broad pulled the gun on me."

"Trust me, you did."

"Yeah, well, compared to what you look like now, I'm must have looked like Sean Connery."

"Great," he said as he climbed over the front seat and into the wider and more comfortable back seat. "Wake me when we get to Denny's, 007."

Chapter 55

Early the next morning he returned to the house in north Seattle. When he discovered that Nora had been arrested he threw a fit. He pushed over furniture, smashed several doors and put holes in a number of walls throughout the house. Again his life was turned upside down because of his incessant desire for heroin. He should have been there with her instead of scoring, but he had to score and that was the catch-22 in his life.

"They would never have taken either one of us alive," he mumbled as he walked through the oak-trimmed halls of the house. He made several calls and within an hour Frank, Linda, Joey and Patty were at the house. He explained to them what had happened and what he planned to do.

"That's pretty risky, don't you think?"

"Risky? Shit, life is risky. No one would believe we had the balls to even try something like this."

"But who's going to get the money to the bail bond's man to free her?" asked Joey.

"That's where Patty comes in."

"But Patty's on probation for a previous rap," Joey protested. " If she's caught with anything illegal she's back to the joint. Then what happens to my kids?"

Patty interrupted, "No, Joey, it's something I want to do. She's my sister, what else can I do?"

Joey didn't like the idea but he begrudgingly conceded to Patty's wishes.

"Fine! It's settled then. Frank, we need a cool place to hide out at for the next few days, got any ideas?"

"Sure. I've got a buddy up in Snohomish County that will put us up. No questions asked. In fact, he might even give us a hand."

"Good. Set it up today. The rest of you come with me."

The group followed Johnny to a storage facility north of the house in Edmonds, a quiet little community on the Puget Sound coast just south of Everett. He had rented the unit to store the proceeds of all the crimes they had committed. It was filled with guns, jewelry, TV's, stereos, tapes and an assortment of odds and ends that had been relieved from their original owners. Now that Nora had been arrested things would have to change. After they managed her release from jail, they were going to have to move fast. Everything had to be ready to go on a dime's notice. He told the group to gather everything they needed from the storage shed. Once that was accomplished they drove up to the Shoreline area and met Frank just south of the Snohomish County line. They followed him to a residence in Mays Pond, a small middle class suburban development southeast of the city of Everett.

It always made Johnny laugh at the thought of settling down when he drove through areas like this. Street after street of split level homes. Some with fences some without, some with a few more trees or better landscaping than their neighbors, but other than the color (which didn't vary much either) they were virtually clones of one another. He couldn't bear to think of himself cooped up in one of these for very long. It would be almost as bad as being back in the joint.

The caravan of cars came to a halt on a tree-lined street filled with the clone-like split-levels he abhorred. He peered out through the windshield of his car at the house, an inconspicuous light blue split-level, where two small children were playing on the front lawn, while a woman in shorts and a T-shirt was mowing the unfenced back yard.

Frank was the first to exit the three cars. As he did, a man in his late forties, with salt and pepper hair and beard, came out of the house and greeted him. The woman stopped mowing the lawn and came up front to see who had arrived. They passed a few pleasantries, and then Frank turned and motioned for Johnny to pull into the driveway. When Johnny pulled in, Joey pulled his van up in front of the house and turned off the engine. They got out of their cars and Frank introduced everyone.

Tucker and Karen Noll had lived in the Mays Pond community for almost five years now. Previously from Salt Lake City, they had moved with their two children to the Seattle area when Tucker had a slight problem with the law after a semi load of stolen property just happened to show up at his house one afternoon while he was "working." It had taken some time and quite a lot of their resources to hire good enough attorneys to get him off, but they succeeded. They found that the atmosphere around Salt Lake after that incident had become a bit too hot for them, so they decided to move to the Northwest. Tucker was one of many out of state transplants currently working as a machinist for Boeing in Everett. He had managed to avert any confrontations with the local police since he had gotten to Seattle, but that did not necessarily mean he had given up his old habits. Karen, on the other hand, was a stay home mother, who knew exactly how Tucker made his "extra" money, and, quite frankly, didn't care, as long as the children were not involved. Tucker's connection with Frank…well, someone had to drive that semi to his house! Later that evening, when Frank explained what had happened and what was going on, both were ripe for the picking and agreed to help.

The very next morning Johnny and Tucker drove back to the Aurora Ave area in south Edmonds in Tucker's green

Oldsmobile. Tucker rented a large storage locker in his name. Once the locker was rented Tucker drove Johnny to a small used car lot where Johnny asked Tucker to buy a white Ford van off the lot. Tucker, not suspecting anything would go awry with their plans, purchased the van in his name with the cash Johnny gave him. They returned to the storage locker and placed the van along with several guns, some jewelry, and clothing and assorted odds and ends in the locker; about half of the things they had removed from the other storage shed the day before. The rest was left in Tuckers downstairs room where Hardy, Frank and Linda were staying. Then, before they left, Johnny took a pad lock he was carrying and locked the door. As they headed back north toward Tucker's house, Johnny finally confided that this would be their escape vehicle in several days when it was time to get out of the area. Not totally happy with the thought of Johnny and his gang leaving the area in a car owned by him, the wheels in Tucker's head began to spin a tale he could use to protect himself and Karen in case anything should go wrong. In the mean time, he had bought in, so he needed to make sure everything went right.

When Tucker and Johnny returned, they rehashed the plans for the next day with everyone at the house. The first thing they decided was that they needed two additional people to be sure they covered all escape routes. Tucker new exactly who to call. About forty-five minutes later, John Ludnick, a work associate of Tucker's and his girlfriend, Susan Kearson, showed up at the house. Tucker spoke with Ludnick on numerous occasions about his "background" and Ludnick had repeatedly told him that if anything came up he should give him a call. Ludnick, in his mid-twenties, good-looking and extremely impressionable, was captivated by the tales of cops and robbers and did not really grasp the magnitude of the situation he was now becoming involved in. His girlfriend, Susan, a twenty-one-year-old blazing redhead, looked a lot smarter than she really was, and for that reason it was decided she would be told only what she needed to know and nothing more.

All nine people left the residence in Mays Pond late that morning and drove to a small nondescript house in Carnation. When they arrived at the house, Johnny assigned everyone to a certain task. Each person was given a map and directions and told what to do. Then the group proceeded to do a dry run of the robbery. As the cars pulled out of the driveway in Carnation to their appointed positions neither Ludnick nor Kearson noticed the blue Dodge Diplomat following them at a distance.

Chapter 56

For the last two days Grogen and Green of the north pro-active squad had been checking the little uninhabited white house in the Carnation area two to three times a day. This morning was no different except for one thing…the house was packed with people. When they drove by, they observed five cars in the driveway and at least nine or ten people, male and female, milling in and around the house. The area being far too rural for them to just blend in they decided to drive east past the house and find a vantage point further up the road where they could monitor what was going on. Less than a quarter mile up the road, they found a driveway to an old abandon barn. From there they could observe everyone through binoculars. As they watched, the people gathered around the front porch of the house and seemed to be listening to the tall man talking from the top step. His animated movements led them to believe that he was directing people to different locations. When he finished speaking everyone got into their cars and began leaving the house. For a moment, they lost sight of all the cars as they exited the driveway one after another. Then one at a time they began to appear, as they separated and went in different directions. Since they could only follow one car at a time they decided to follow the Honda which turned northbound onto the West Snoqualmie

Valley Road and headed toward the Novelty Hill Road. They caught up with the Honda on the Novelty Hill Road where they noticed it was following a yellow station wagon. Both cars continued on the Novelty until about 95th NE and then turned on to the Avondale Road. They went a short distance and then turned around and went back in the same direction. At about NE 204th, both the Honda and the station wagon pulled off to the side of the road. As the officers drove past the cars, they noticed a white male with dark hair and a potbelly get out of the Honda. He walked over to the station wagon and talked to the driver, a white male in his twenties with a slender face and brown hair. In the passenger side of the car was a white female with auburn hair.

Suddenly the radio in their glove box crackled with an emergency message, "All north end units, I'm receiving a 10-33 through a landline that an officer needs help. The address is…"

"Just our luck. Hal, why don't you switch over to the TAC frequency and have them notify DeNucci and Anderson about what's going on while I head for the call."

Grogen picked up the radio and advised dispatch they were responding to the 10-33. Then switched to the TAC frequency and asked the dispatcher to contact the two detectives downtown and ask them for a number they could be reached at.

Because of their quick departure, what Green and Grogen did not see was the male in the Honda picking up a hand-held radio from the front seat of his car and answering a call. Shortly after the radio transmission the two cars pulled back onto the road and disappeared.

Before Grogen and Green could reach the assistance call, the emergency was cancelled. They decided to return to see if the two cars were still there. As luck would have it, they were not. So they decided to head back to the residence in Carnation to see if anyone had returned. When they arrived, the house was as quiet as it had been the previous two days. They waited another half hour and then left.

Five minutes later, Grogen was on a landline to DeNucci explaining what they had just seen.

After going over the entire scenario Bob asked, "You know what it looks like, don't you?"

"Sure do," Grogen replied.

"Thanks for the good work. Keep your eyes open, I'm sure they're planning some sort of surprise."

"Yeah, will do! We'll keep checking the place the next few days during our shift. If thing go to hell in a hand basket, we'll know what to do."

"OK. Tell the other guys in the unit what's going on and thanks again." DeNucci hung up the phone and put his head in his hands. "What are these bastards up to now?"

"What's up, Bobby?" Andy shouted as he walked across the bullpen. "Looks like you had some bad lunch."

"No. Worse! Our friends were just at the house in Carnation and it looks as though they're planning something." Bob filled Andy in on the rest of his conversation with Grogen and then took the envelope that Andy handed him. It was the booking photos of the suspects from the burglary down south. Bob threw the photos into the pile on his desk, picked up the phone and began dialing Rick Reed's number.

Chapter 57

It was a little after two in the afternoon when Johnny and Frank, driven by Tucker in his Olds drove through the little city of Snohomish, a small farming community about forty miles northeast of Seattle, priding itself as the antique capitol of the Northwest. The main street of town looked just like a photograph from the turn-of-the-century with one addition. It was jam- packed with modern-day cars and people who visited the town every day to take advantage of its many antique boutiques and quaint little cafes. This was the perfect spot to find what the three men were looking for. As they drove through the main part of town, their heads pivoted from left to right looking to take advantage of the perfect opportunity when it presented itself. Finally after about fifteen minutes they spotted it. Quickly the men applied their trade and acquired what it was they were looking for. Within minutes they were headed back out of town toward a prearranged meeting place with the rest of the group.

About three o'clock that afternoon, six cars met in a shopping center northeast of Duvall in the little town of Monroe. The blue Ford LTD, driven by Frank's girlfriend Linda; the van with Joey and Patty; the Honda with Ludnick; the yellow station wagon with Kearson; Tucker in the green Olds and Johnny and Frank in the red Mustang they had just stolen not more than a half hour ago.

Earlier that morning, Johnny and Frank drove into the sleepy little town of Duvall to scope out the Sea First Bank. Bookstores, antique shops and quaint boutiques surrounded the bank, a nondescript brick building on the corner of Cherry and Main Street. As they pulled up across the street from the bank they took a few moments to scan the surroundings. While doing so, both Johnny and Frank's attention were drawn to an attractive brunette who just happened to be smoking outside the front doors of the bank. Both men stared more than they should have, considering the fact that this was a small town and anything out of the ordinary might be construed as strange or a threat. The woman seemed to sense their stares and became a little nervous. She quickly put out her cigarette and went into the bank.

Against his better judgment, Johnny dared to go into the bank and approach the manager for information on opening an account. When he entered the front door he immediately noticed the brunette behind a teller window. *Nice going,* he thought to himself. While waiting for information, he sized up the layout of the bank, including the number of tellers and additional employees. He checked to see whether there was a guard on duty and whether there was clear access to the bank vault once they were inside. And last, he made sure the building had an alternate escape route just in case something unforeseen occurred at the front door. Satisfied with what he saw, he thanked the manager for the information and left the bank. When he got back in the car with Frank, he didn't mention the brunette.

There was a buzz of electricity in the air as they gathered at the shopping center. Johnny went over last minute changes. He reminded them, if anything went wrong they were to meet at the safe house in Carnation as quickly as possible. Patty, still sitting in her van and the only one not taking part in the actual robbery, would be at the house, just in case, to provide everyone with alternate ID and a planned route out of town if necessary. What Johnny didn't know was that stashed in the back of Joey and Patty's van was their six-year-old son whom Patty insisted upon bringing. Joey had told her that this was no place for a child, but Patty refused to listen and covered the child with blankets and pillows so no one would be aware of his presence.

When the job was done, Johnny's plan was to dump the Mustang and use Tucker's green Olsmobile. If things didn't go as planned, they would decide at that time which of the other three drivers, Linda, Susan or John, they would meet up with to make their escape. Then he asked Tucker to give him the sport bag he had left in his car. He opened the bag and removed several sets of walkie-talkies. He told all of them to keep a sharp ear on their radios, which he then handed to them, so they would know what was going on. If all went well, they would all find their own way back to the house in Mays Pond.

Then he turned to Tucker and asked, "You up for this?"

"Hell, yes, I'm up for it. Let's get going." Tucker got into his green Olds and started it up. Turning to the others in the parking lot Johnny said, "See you guys in Mays Pond," Then he and Frank sped away in the Mustang.

The rest of the cars scattered from the parking lot in all directions, like mice scurrying from a cat. What they didn't know was that *this* cat was about to pounce.

Chapter 58

Their shift had started slowly that day with coffee, as usual at Denny's in Kenmore, just up the block from the precinct. To Grogen and Green, stuck on day-shift for the next month, it was sheer torture. None of the pro-active officers appreciated working that shift. After all, nothing happened on day-shift except maybe an occasional stolen car report or a burglary report from an entry that occurred the previous evening.

After their morning coffee, both officers returned to the precinct to finish up some old paperwork their boss had been pushing them for. When they got to the precinct they secluded themselves in their office and spent the better part of the morning finishing reports and writing statements on several burglary arrests they made the week before on a different shift.

Bob and Andy's day wasn't going much better. Because of their case load it was necessary to finish up dictating several statements that were needed by the prosecutor for a case due in court the following week. The difference between being a pro-active officer at the precinct level and a detective downtown was that downtown you didn't have to write your own statements or reports. All that was needed was for you to dictate your statement into your tape recorder and give the tape to the ladies in the typing pool who would then transcribe it for you. Andy had just finished with his statement when he received a phone call from Kelly Egan at the Seattle Police Department.

"Hey, you Swedish faggot. What's goin' on?"

Immediately recognizing the voice, he responded, "You big ugly Irish bastard. What the hell do you want?"

After the pleasantries were completed Egan gave Andy the news. "You remember that hunch you and your partner had about that slug found at that Redmond robbery? Well, it paid off. I just got the ballistics report back from the lab and the slug they pulled out of the alarm in Redmond is a perfect match to the slug taken from the victim at my restaurant robbery."

"Great. I'll pass on the news. You gonna be in this afternoon?"

"When aren't I in the office?"

"Well if Bob wants to talk to you about the slug, I'll have him call you."

"Terrific, just what I need, another Italian lesson," Kelly laughed and hung up the phone.

Bob finished his statement and dropped it off at the front desk. As he left the desk, he couldn't help but look down over the counter at the long legs of the receptionist protruding like two bolts of silk from a short tight miniskirt that barely covered her thighs. He now understood why Andy spent most of his mornings up front. When he returned to his desk Andy gave him the news about the slug. The connection between the two crimes spurred him on to think of the other crimes they had already connected them to. He began to think about how many crimes in the area might be attributed to this group. He didn't know now, but he certainly was going to find out.

Suddenly his train of thought was broken by a female voice calling his name from the front office.

"Bob DeNucci. Pick up your radio. North Precinct dispatch is trying to reach you!"

Bob groped around his desk momentarily to find the portable radio. When he did he heard the broadcast to units in the North Precinct.

"Be advised all eastside units we've just received a call of a reported armed robbery at the Sea First Bank in Duvall. There's a preliminary report of at least two suspects wearing makeup and wigs. Additional information to follow."

Bob's brain kicked into high gear. In a split second he knew these were their guys. He needed time to think, but something in the back of his mind told him that there had to be a connection between the bank and Nora, the girl they had just arrested. He pulled open the top drawer of his desk and grabbed his . 9mm Smith and Wesson.

"It's them," he said to Andy, "Let's go."

Andy grabbed his own gun and holster from his desk and followed Bob out of the bullpen to their car.

As Bob catapulted from his chair, gun and holster in hand, he had a second thought. He stopped and quickly returned to his desk where he grabbed the booking photos Andy had given him. If his hunch paid off this could be the break they were waiting for.

Chapter 59

The red Mustang cruised southbound on Highway 203 between Monroe and Duvall with the green Oldsmobile close behind. As they entered the town of Duvall, the Mustang pulled over to the side of the road in front of the Duvall Tavern to allow the Olds to pass. Tucker, in the Olds, continued southbound out of town until he reached the Big Rock Road where, after a glance in the rear view mirror to make sure he wasn't being followed, he took a left. He cruised east bound up the Big Rock Road, about three hundred yards east of the highway, until he found the almost invisible entrance to the dirt road Johnny had showed him the day before. Tucker pulled the Olds into the branch and vine covered driveway and drove about fifty yards until he came to a small turn around. He turned the Olds around and waited.

For Jennie Johnson, Rhonda Bards and Terri Baylor, the day was just another day at work at the Duvall branch of the Sea First Bank. The three women, though not close in age, had become close friends while working at the bank. From the first week all three worked at the bank together it became apparent they all shared an interest in antiques. And for the past year, once a week, the three would venture out into the adjoining farming and dairy communities and hunt for their favorite pieces. This week would be no different. At five o'clock that afternoon, when the bank closed, the three women would begin their quest for their own holy grail of the week.

The first sign this was not another ordinary day came about 10:30 that morning when Jennie had stepped outside the front doors of the bank to take in and enjoy a beautiful Northwest morning. She had just lit up a cigarette when she became aware of two men parked across the street from the bank in a blue Ford. Both men stared at her for a few minutes. Feeling rather uneasy about the situation, she put out her cigarette and returned to the bank. A few minutes later, after she took her place in the teller cage, one to the men entered the bank. He was tall, about six feet, with sandy brown hair. He was wearing a plaid shirt, jeans and tennis shoes and a pair of mirrored sunglasses which he never removed the entire time he was in the bank. While the man spoke with Brian Ewing, the bank manager, Jennie leaned over into the adjoining cage where Terri Baylor worked and told her about the two men. Both women watched as the sandy-haired man in sunglasses shook the manager's hand and left the bank. Then Terri, the older and more experienced of the two tellers walked over to the manager.

"What did he want?"

"What did who want? Oh, you mean the gentleman that was just here? He wanted some information on opening an account with our bank."

"Opening an account or making a withdrawal?" Terri asked seriously.

Ewing caught the tone in her voice and immediately asked her to explain what she was implying. Terri relayed what Jennie had told her about the two men and suggested that they at least try and get a license plate off the car before it left its parking spot across the street. But before they could get out the door the blue Ford was two blocks away and the plate was impossible to see.

It was four o'clock when the red Mustang and its two occupants pulled up to the corner of Main and Cherry in Duvall. The car was left running as the two men got out and entered the bank. Johnny, wearing a burnt orange sport jacket, black gloves and a straw type cowboy hat with a feather, entered first. His face was neatly covered with dark pancake makeup, a dark wig, a mustache and his mirrored sunglasses. Frank dressed in a brown sport jacket, brown hat and gloves and sporting a mustache and goatee along with a blond wig, followed close behind.

The first person to see them come through the front door was Jennie. Because of her age and inexperience, she was startled by their appearance. Before she could recover, Johnny hurled himself over the teller cage and with gun in hand, ordered all three tellers onto the floor. Meanwhile, Frank was busy screaming at the three bank customers and the bank manager to lie down on the floor. Everyone followed their orders and in the confusion that followed no one hit the silent alarm button.

This time, while the tellers lay face-down on the floor of the bank, Johnny emptied the teller drawers into white canvas bank bags he found behind the counter, careful not to include the explosive packages contained in each of the drawers. When he was done emptying the cash drawers, he grabbed Jennie by the hair, picked her up off the floor and demanded the keys to the vault area. Jennie began to tell him that she didn't have the keys when she felt the back of his hand across her face. The impact from Johnny's blow took her by surprise and knocked her off her feet. Johnny reached down and grabbed her by the front of her sweater ripping off three buttons and revealing a white lace bra beneath. She got to her feet pulling her ripped sweater closed over her exposed breasts and not knowing what else to do, she began to cry. Before Johnny could unleash another attack upon her, Terri Baylor sprang to her feet and grabbed the young girl who was now sobbing uncontrollably.

Johnny walked up to Terri and placed his gun to her temple. "I want the keys to the vault, and I want them now."

Terri extended her arm toward Johnny. He grabbed the key chain from her hand then ordered both women to the floor once more. He entered the bank vault and a short time later returned holding several metal boxes containing money and other valuables he had taken from the vault.

He called Frank over to the teller cages and handed him the two metal boxes. Then he picked up the three canvas bags filled with bills and both men headed out the front door of the bank.

At 3:55,Tucker put the Oldsmobile in gear, pulled out onto the Big Rock Road and headed for the highway back to town. At about five after four Tucker pulled up to the intersection of Fourth and Taylor in Duvall. As he did, the Mustang screeched to a halt beside his car and two men emerged carrying bank bags and strong boxes. The two men relieved themselves of their disguises, quickly threw the bags and boxes into the Olds and got in. Tucker pulled away from the intersection while the two men lie on the floor in the back of the car. As he drove away he looked in his rear view mirror and saw the Mustang, in neutral and running, straddling the intersection with both doors wide open. They were safely out of town on the other side of the valley before they heard the faint sound of police sirens responding to the bank alarm.

Chapter 60

Grogen and Green were just about ready to call it a day. They had finished their reports and were in the parking lot with their second-shift replacements when the robbery tone blared from their portable radio. Both men listened as the dispatcher broadcast a robbery at the Duvall branch of the Seattle First Bank.

Without as much as a word, both men bolted to their unmarked car and sped eastbound from the parking lot toward the Duvall/Carnation area, leaving the two second-shift officers just arriving for work to wonder what it was they had missed about the call. Grogen picked up the car radio and asked the dispatcher to contact DeNucci or Anderson downtown and get them on the radio ASAP. Several minutes passed before Grogen, now on the TAC frequency, received his call.

"Are you downtown or on the road?" Grogen asked.

"We're on the road coming your way," Andy replied.

"Did you hear the radio call?"

"Yeah. We received the info from dispatch and are headed that way."

"You know where we're headed, don't you?"

"We sure do. Good hunting. We'll see you shortly." Andy put down his radio and looked over at Bob. "Well what do you know. Maybe, just maybe we've caught a break on this one."

When Grogen finished on the radio his adrenaline was pumping. He reached into his jacket pocket, pulled out a pack of Marlboro and lit one up.

"Do me a favor and open your window so I don't have to breathe that shit," Green pleaded to his partner.

He cracked open the passenger window of the car then turned to his partner and smiled. "I've been around for a while and I've never had a jump on the scum bags like this. Am I dreaming?"

"Not likely. 'Cause if you are, we're both having the same dream," Green replied with a laugh.

"You know, this is what makes this job so much fun."

"Yeah, well don't let it go to your head. You know what we're looking for. Now let's find it."

In order to reach their car, Bob and Andy had to pass through an underground tunnel that connected the courthouse with the County Administration Building and the garage. The two men ran through the tunnel and up to the garage where their car was parked on the second floor. It was Bob's day to drive. As soon as they left the covered parking, Andy was on the radio. He contacted Grogen and Green then called dispatch and asked them to contact Kelly Egan and Rick Reed. Both men agreed to meet them in the Duvall area as soon as they could get there.

Chapter 61

The sirens faded as they continued west on the Woodinville Duvall Highway. When the green Oldsmobile containing the three men reached Paradise Lake Road, it turned northbound and headed toward Snohomish County and the safety of Tucker's home. Meanwhile, the others headed for their contact points in anticipation of a radio call that never came.

Not being from the Seattle area, Susan Kearson became easily separated from her boyfriend in the Honda. She had not driven the station wagon the day before so she was unfamiliar with many of the roads. Within minutes of losing site of her boyfriend, she was wandering aimlessly on the Novelty and Avondale Roads. She momentarily pulled into the parking lot of the Avondale Market on NE 116th and then pulled back out onto the Avondale and drove back to the Novelty Hill Road. As she traveled down the Novelty, she became nervous and uneasy and decided to try to find her way back to Tucker's house in Mays Pond. Using a hand-drawn map she had received the day before from Frank, she headed north on the West Snoqualmie Valley Road and then turned west on the Woodinville Duvall Road.

Grogen and Green were traveling east on the Novelty Road when they spotted the yellow station wagon going in the opposite direction. They notified radio, then turned around and followed it. From about five car lengths behind, they watched as the wagon went north on the Avondale Road to the Avondale Market, pulled in the lot and then quickly pulled back out on the Avondale in the opposite direction. As the car exited the market, it crossed in front of their car. Both officers saw the red head they had seen the previous day, driving the wagon. Green turned their car around and caught up with the wagon on the Novelty Hill Road. Within a few minutes, the car was headed up the Woodinville Duvall toward the Avondale. Grogen pulled the Kojak light from beneath the front seat, plugged it in and threw it on the dashboard of their car. The station wagon pulled to the shoulder of the road and stopped. Grogen was out of the car first and approached the wagon on the passenger side with his gun drawn, while Green walked cautiously up to the driver's door, hand on the butt of his gun, which was unsnapped in his holster. Susan Kearson rolled down the driver's side window and looked up at Green.

"Yes, Officer, did I do something wrong?"

"May I see your license and the registration to your vehicle?" he asked while cautiously checking out the back seat of the car.

"I'm sorry, but a friend of mine loaned the car to me today and I don't know where the registration is."

"How about some identification, miss?"

"My purse is in the back of the car by the rear hatch."

Green asked her if she would give him permission to go into the car, get her purse and then look through her car. Kearson agreed and handed Green the keys. Grogen, whose presence Kearson was still not aware of, stood on the passenger side of the vehicle with his gun drawn. Green opened the hatchback of the wagon and retrieved her purse. When he returned to the driver's door, he asked her to step out of the car. When Kearson got out, Green escorted her to the passenger side of the car where Grogen stood with his gun still drawn. She remained there while Green opened the passenger side door and looked in. He didn't open the glove box, but knelt on the front seat and flipped down the visor on the driver's side of the car. Three sheets of folded green-lined paper floated down on the seat in front of him. He picked up the first sheet and unfolded it. There, drawn on the creased green paper, was a hand drawn map of the Duvall area with a large "X" over the Sea First Bank.

"I think I've seen just about enough," Green said as he exited the car, locked all the doors and called for a tow truck to bring the car to the police impound lot. Once they had the car under police control at the lot they would do the paperwork for a search warrant and process the car for any additional evidence. Later that evening when they served the warrant on the car they found a total of three separate maps of the Duvall area all marked with an "X" on the Sea First Bank location.

By this time, Kearson was in tears. Grogen took her by the arm and led her back to their car. He asked her to take off her coat, then quickly checking the waistband of her pants, placed her in handcuffs and put her in the back seat of their unmarked patrol car.

Chapter 62

The two detectives in the brown Dodge Diplomat sped eastbound across the Interstate 90 floating bridge, the second of the two bridges that spanned Lake Washington linking the downtown Seattle area with the affluent east side. As they reached the west side of the bridge, Bob picked up the radio and called for Grant Seward, one of the second-shift pro-active officers that was involved in the stake-out of the house on Aurora. When he reached him they both switched over to the TAC frequency.

"Grant, this is Bob. I need you to do us a favor."

"Sure. Go ahead."

"We're headed out to the Duvall area on that robbery and need someone to keep an eye on a house we think the bad guys are using."

"I know the one. I talked to Hal yesterday."

"Good. If there's anyone else that can go with you, it might be a good idea."

"No problem, I've got Benson workin' with me. We're on our way."

"Thanks, we owe you one."

"I know you do. And believe me, you'll pay." He placed the radio down, grinned at Benson and said, "Time to go to work, partner."

Seward and Benson, who shortly before were left in the dust by Grogen and Green, pulled out of the precinct parking lot and headed east on Bothell Way toward the Duvall area. Because rush hour was beginning, they chose to go east past Woodinville, turn on Paradise Lake Road and head towards Duvall. As they approached the Woodinville Duvall Road, they saw the tow truck and the yellow station wagon. Grogen, Green and their guest were in their unmarked vehicle behind the wagon following it to the precinct lot. In this manner they could continue the chain of evidence by following the tow truck back to the precinct where the car would be parked in a secure area while they secured the warrant.

Seward and his partner drove down the Woodinville Duvall Road and before going across the valley, turned south on Snoqualmie Valley Road. About a block from the old white house, he found the same deserted driveway that Grogen and Green had used the previous day and pulled in and waited. Ten minutes later, a van pulled into the driveway of the house and a male got out and went in. A short time later, the officers heard shots coming from the direction of the house. Seward picked up his binoculars and observed a male, wearing a black and white ball cap, firing a silver handgun in the front yard, out by the road. With the help of his binoculars, Seward was able to pull the license plate number off the back of the van. When it was run for information, it came back to a Joey and Patti Mendosa of Seattle.

On closer inspection through his binoculars, Seward could see that the male firing the weapon was definitely of Mexican heritage. He finished firing the gun as fast as he started then went back into the house. A few minutes later the same man accompanied by a woman and child exited the house and got into the van. Unknown to the two officers, the man reached over and placed the Ruger he had been firing back into the glove box, the same place it had been since the day he had taken it from the car at the airport parking lot. He started the van and backed it out of the driveway, then headed straight for the two officers in their car. Joey noticed the car too late to avoid eye contact with the two officers as he drove by. Benson got on the radio and called for DeNucci and Anderson.

"We've got a male, female and child in a van that just left the house. The male was firing a gun in the front yard just before they left."

"Let's switch over to TAC," Andy asked Benson. Then to the radio dispatcher he said, "Radio, close down TAC and advise all units involved in this incident to switch over to TAC for all radio transmissions."

"Copy"

"You have any back-up close?" Andy asked the two officers.

A uniform officer cut in. "Affirmative. Boy 3 responding from about a mile away."

Then the pro-active sergeant chimed in, "Two David responding from the Duvall area. Be there in about two or three."

"OK," said Andy. "We're approaching NE 124th Street in Kirkland, we'll head your way. When you get some back up go ahead and take him."

Seward pulled out of the driveway behind the van as it passed. Joey, sensing what was about to happen, panicked and pulled into the next driveway he came to. Not wanting to make a stop on the suspect's terms, the officers drove past the driveway and up the road around a bend where he pulled off onto the gravel. There they were met by Sgt. Jake Reed, their boss. Reed pulled up alongside the unmarked car just as the van, came around the bend in the road with the marked unit, Boy 3, right behind him.

Chapter 63

On the ride back to the precinct, Grogen had dispatch contact the FBI, currently en route to the bank in Duvall, and advise them of what they had. Dispatch got back to Grogen shortly after and advised him that an agent would be responding to the precinct within the hour. When they arrived at the precinct with Kearson, they immediately took her inside. While Green and Grogen went to their office to wait for the FBI agent, Kearson was patted down and searched by a female officer then placed in a holding cell. Over an hour passed and no agent had shown up. Green and Grogen decided that valuable information could be slipping away, so they decided to conduct the interview with Kearson with or without the feds.

When the two officers went to remove Kearson from the cell, they could see that she was upset. Her face was flushed and covered with tears. The mascara from both her bloodshot eyes streaked her puffy cheeks as she was pacing the small ten-by-ten cell. They brought her to the pro-active office, sat her down and Green offered her a Coke he purchased earlier. She opened the Coke and took a large gulp. Then she placed the cap back on the bottle, placed the bottle on the desk in front of her and spoke her first words since being take into custody.

"I didn't have anything to do with this whole thing. My boyfriend called me up the other day and asked me to help him and his friends out. I said that I would, so yesterday we drove to this house by Duvall and met with some other people. I don't even know their names. I was given several maps and they showed me where to go and wait until I received a call."

"How were you going to get a call?" asked Green.

"They gave me a small portable radio. It's under my seat in the car. But I never got any call. Matter of fact, I never got to where I was going. I got lost. I don't come from this area, you see. And," she stopped to wipe the tears from her eyes, "I think I made a couple of wrong turns. But I never heard from anyone. I swear."

"What were you supposed to do when they called you?"

"I think just wait to see if someone needed a ride."

"Well, where did you think this someone was coming from?" Green continued, a little more forcefully than he probably should have.

Kearson burst into tears and began to sob uncontrollably. They let her cry for a few minutes and then this time Grogen stepped in.

"Do you think your boyfriend would know who these people are?"

Between sobs, Kearson answered. "Yes...I'm...sure he...would."

"Where can we find your boyfriend now? And what's his name?"

"John...John Ludnick." She was beginning to calm down now. "I don't know where he is right now, but you could try his apartment in Bellevue."

Green copied down the address and phone number that she gave them. A few minutes later after placing Kearson back in the holding cell, he was headed to the phone to call Ludnick. Before he could pick up the phone to call, the PA system in the precinct crackled with a message that a male was on line one inquiring about their female prisoner.

Green grabbed the phone in his office and punched line one. "Hello, Green here."

"Hello, I'm calling to find out if you have a young girl by the name of Kearson at the precinct."

"May I ask who's calling?" Green played along, knowing full well who the caller must be.

"This is just a friend. I was told that she had been arrested. Can I speak with her?"

"Who might have told you that she was arrested." Green paused. "John?"

That last bit of information caused the caller to stop and hold his breath.

"John," Green continued, "I know this is you. We have your girlfriend here at the precinct and, quite honestly, I don't think she's very involved in this thing. What do you think?"

"Look, she really didn't know what the hell was going on. She just was doing me a favor. She isn't guilty of anything except maybe of being naive."

"I realize that, John. But we're gonna have to have you come down here and talk to us about this whole thing."

"No way, man, I come down there and you'll arrest me on the spot. I didn't have anything to do with the robbery, but you guys will arrest me anyway."

"John, the only way we can clear this up is to have you come down here."

"No! If you want me to clear things up for you, I can do it over the phone. I'm not coming in."

Green didn't want to tip him off to the fact that they knew where he lived. If they were going to get this guy, they were going to have to play stupid.

"OK, John. Tell you what. I'll contact my supervisor to OK this phone thing. Right now he's in Duvall. He should be here in about a half hour. Why don't you call me back in about a half hour and we'll take care of this. Then we can release your girlfriend. Fair enough?"

John thought for a moment and then replied, "A half hour? Alright, I call you back in a half hour." He hung up.

Green ran to the office and got Grogen. Then both men raced out to their car and headed for the Bellevue address. They had just a half hour to fight the rush hour traffic and find the address before their man disappeared.

Chapter 64

"Take him, Ron," Seward said as he, Benson and Reed pulled in behind the marked unit.

With his emergency lights flashing, the officer pulled the van over just before it turned up NE 124 toward the Novelty Hill Road. Joey pulled the van over and told Patti to stay put. He got out of the vehicle and tried to walk back to talk to the officers. He had taken only two steps from the van when Seward grabbed him by the shirt and spun him around against the van. Benson, on the passenger side of the van, opened Patti's door and asked her to get out and give him some identification.

"You have the right to remain silent. Anything you say, can and will be used against you in a court of law..." Grant continued with his rights. When he concluded, he removed Joey's wallet from his back pocket and took out his license. Seward took the portable radio from his own jacket pocket and gave the dispatcher Joey and Patti's information for a warrant check. With the information given and the driver and passenger identified, he turned Joey around and to talk to him about the robbery.

"What do you know about any robbery in the area today, Joey?" he asked.

"I didn't rob any bank, man," Joey blurted.

"Who said anything about a bank, Joey? You have a guilty conscious?"

Joey whispered an "Oh shit" under his breath then sighed out loud. "Hey, man, what do you want? I didn't do nothin'."

"That looked like a pretty good-looking gun you had there, Joey," said Reed, now standing shoulder-to-shoulder with Seward. "You still have it on you?"

"What gun are you talkin' about, man?"

Just then the radio blared. "David four five, do you have both of those individuals in custody?"

"That's affirmative, radio. We're havin' a nice little chat right now."

"Be advised there's no active on the male but he's got a rap sheet as long as a roll of toilet paper. We have a hit on the female. Two misdemeanor warrants out of Shoreline district court for shoplifting."

The frame of Jake Reed eclipsed the sun as he stepped in front of Grant Seward and grabbed Joey by his shirt. Before Reed could say another word, DeNucci and Anderson pulled up at the scene.

"I'll be back, asshole, don't go away," Jake said as he released Joey's shirt long enough to turn and greet both detectives.

"Hi, guys," he said with a wink and a smile, "I think we've got a couple of keepers."

Both DeNucci and Anderson were anxious to speak with the occupants of the van. But before doing so, Andy answered a radio call from Kelly Egan.

"Go ahead, Kelly."

"Does the male half of your stop fit the description of our restaurant shooter?"

Anderson took a good look at Joey, and then got back on the radio.

"Not the shooter but he sure could be the second guy. He's not going anywhere for a while. Why don't you come by our location and have a chat with him."

"I'll be there in about fifteen."

Chapter 65

They reached the Bellevue address with five minutes to spare. There parked outside the apartment in the parking lot was the Honda identified with the bank robbery. Green parked the car in the complex parking lot and they waited.

Meanwhile, the phone rang at the precinct and was answered by the receptionist at the front desk.

"No, Officer Green in not at the precinct right now. I don't know where he's gone. He left about a half hour ago."

When he hung up the phone his head was spinning. What was going on? Where was that officer? Then, as if a light bulb had gone on, he knew exactly what was happening. He grabbed his jacket and keys and dashed out the door of his apartment. Running down the staircase and out the door, he headed straight for his car in the parking lot of the apartment complex. As he reached the car, he took out his keys and placed them in the door lock.

"Hello, John," a familiar voice whispered in his ear.

He felt the cold steel barrel of Green's service revolver pressed against the back of his head. A wave of nausea swept over his body. His shoulders slumped; he dropped his jacket then bent over and puked on his own shoes.

Chapter 66

Bob and Andy got out of their car and walked over to the group of officers that had now grown to about six, surrounding the van. Seward filled them in on what they had and it was decided they would separate the driver and passenger and speak with each separately. Andy placed Joey in handcuffs and walked him back to his car.

Grant and Benson led Patti and the boy they found in the back of the van to Jake Reed's unmarked cruiser. Although it was customary for anyone placed in their back seat to be handcuffed, due to the fact that she was with her six-year-old child, the officers decided that they would not follow the normal procedure. Benson called over one of the female uniformed officers presently at their location and asked her to do a thorough pat-down and search of the female prisoner. When that was complete and they were all satisfied that Patti had no contraband or anything else that would endanger them, she was put in the back seat with her son.

Before Bob got in his car with Joey, he walked over and grabbed Grant by the arm and pulled him aside. "Don't go anywhere with the girl and the kid. I've got an idea."

Before Bob returned to his car, he went to the van to get the ownership papers from the glove box. If they were lucky it would be stolen and maybe they would have some leverage on this dirt bag. He opened the passenger side door, reached in and opened the glove box. To his surprise, out fell a chrome-plated Ruger. He took the Ruger from the van, walked back to his car and got in with Andy and Joey. Jake Reed saw Bob take the gun from the van and joined him at the car. Andy advised Joey of his rights while Jake slid into the back with him. When he finished with the Miranda warnings, they began their interrogation.

"So, Joey, this is a pretty big piece of equipment. Does it belong to you?" Bob asked.

"What are you talking about man?"

"Come on, Joey. Where do you think I pulled this thing from, my ass?" Bob said sarcastically as he emptied the chrome revolver, turned in his seat and held it up.

"I don't know what you're talkin' about, man. I ain't never seen that before."

Jake reached over and grabbed Joey by the shirt. "I told you we weren't done yet, asshole. Now the detective asked you where the gun came from. I think you should answer him."

"You know I can't do that. I'm a dead man if I do."

Bob interjected, "You're damned if you do and damned if you don't, Joey. Why don't I try to make the decision a little easier for you and add a little bit more to the ante?"

Reed seemed to sense what Bob had in mind and immediately released Joey's shirt and leaned back.

"What do you mean?" Joey asked.

"What I mean is right now, over in that other police car, we've got your wife and son. Now your wife has got a couple of warrants for her arrest, and I bet, I'm just guessing, mind you, but I bet if I were to check, she probably has a couple of felony raps. Isn't that so?"

Joey nodded.

"And you know if she's a felon, she's probably got a parole officer." Bob waited to get a nod from Joey then continued. "What do you think will happen to her if she got caught with a gun, a loaded gun, and I bet even a stolen loaded gun? She would probably be headed straight back to the joint. What do you think?"

"Oh, man, you're a cold-blooded son-of-a-bitch!" Then when Bob didn't respond he continued, "You ain't really gonna send her back, are you?" Joey continued to whine. "We got kids now, you know."

Bingo! They had found the weak link.

"I know, Joey, and I'd hate to see those kids taken out of your home and sent to foster care while both their parents went to jail. Wouldn't you?"

Joey shook his head and slumped down in the back seat of the car.

"Oh, man, you're a cold son-of-a-bitch," he repeated. "You know I could get offed for this."

"I can get a lot colder if you won't cooperate, Joey. But on the other hand, if you want to cooperate, I'm sure we can work something out." The trap was baited. Now let's see if the animal bites.

With a sigh of resignation Joey looked up at DeNucci. "What do you want?"

"What I want, Joey, is the guy behind today's bank robbery. And if I'm right, behind a lot of crimes that have gone on around this area and others for quite a while. I want his name and want you to set him up for us."

"And what do I get out of the deal?"

"If, and I do mean if, you deliver me the big fish and the other guppies, you and Patti walk."

Joey lifted his head and look directly at Bob. "I turn this guy and his friends for you and we walk, no questions asked?"

All three men agreed it was worth turning a blind eye to Joey and his wife if they could get the man and the group behind all of this mayhem. Bob turned back to Joey and repeated emphatically, "No questions asked and you and Patti walk."

Joey thought back to that night at the Chinese restaurant. Johnny had demeaned and mocked him. He had sworn that night that he would pay him back for that. Now was his chance, and payback was a bitch. He would be the one in control of Johnny's destiny, not the other way around. A big smile crept across his face as he answered Bob, "You've got a deal."

"One other thing," Bob said as he turned in his seat and faced Joey. "Just in case you have any thoughts of double-crossing us in this deal, Patti and your son are going to be taken to the precinct where we're going to hold them until you come through with your end of the bargain. You deliver, they go free. It's the best *and only* deal in town at the moment."

Joey nodded his head in agreement. Jake got out of the car and told Bob and Andy he'd take care of the arrangements with Seward and Benson. Then he would join them if they didn't mind.

While the sergeant made arrangements with the other officers to take Patti and her son to the precinct, Bob and Andy proceeded with their interrogation of Joey.

"OK, Joey, what's our guy's name?'

"His name is Johnny Hardy."

"Hardy!" Anderson almost choked on his own words, "Do you know who?"

Bob interrupted him, "I know exactly who." Then turning toward Joey he said, "Joey, are you sure this guy is Hardy?"

"Am I sure? Fuckin-A, I'm sure. The son-of-a-bitch is married to Patti's sister Nora. That's what the bank job was all about...getting the money to bail out Nora."

"I knew there had to be a connection between the two," Bob said to Andy. "Where is Hardy now?"

"I'm not sure exactly where he is, but I've got a number he gave me to reach him. I can call it and set up a meeting."

"Before you do, Joey, tell me about the Ruger." Bob had already run the serial number on the gun and was waiting for the dispatcher to come back with some information. He continued questioning Joey, "Where did you get it?"

Joey's heart sank. He knew he should have listened to Johnny and ditched the gun the day he took it from the van. Now it would be the downfall of both of them.

"It's Hardy's," he said. "I don't remember how long ago it was, but he called me and asked me if I would go to the airport and pick the gun up from a van he had left it in, then ditch it in the Sound. Obviously I didn't ditch it," he replied disgustingly.

"What was the gun doing in the van," Bob pried a bit more, "had he used it anywhere?"

Just then the dispatcher came on the radio and advised Bob that the gun had been stolen two years ago during a burglary where the victim was murdered. Bob turned to ask Joey about this change in circumstances, but before he could get a word out, Joey blurted, "No way, man. I had no idea about that." Then as nonchalant as a person asking to pass the sugar, Joey said, "Besides, Hardy used this gun in his escape from jail."

Both men were totally caught off-guard at the casual way Joey had made this last statement. This was the gun that had killed the corrections officer in Hardy's escape! "Just another link in this big ugly chain," Bob thought out loud. Now more than ever they knew they had to stop this madman.

Before they could acknowledge the last transmission from dispatch, Kelly Egan and Rick Reed pulled up to their location. Andy got out of the car and talked to both men.

"Hello, Kelly. Hey, Rick." He took both men a short distance away from the car and began an explanation of what had gone on so far.

"We've got a live one in there with Bob. Our perp's name is Hardy, Johnny Hardy. Either of you remember him?"

"Hardy!" Kelly answered first. "You don't mean that dirt bag bastard that shot the jail guard at Harborview Medical Center during an escape a year or so ago?"

"The same dirt bag."

"That son-of-a-bitch had the balls to come back to this state? Hell, this town. I can't believe it. Why the hell would he do something like that?"

"No one ever said crime and intelligence go together. Who knows why he came back, but he's back. And not only that, he's back with the same gun he killed the corrections officer with when he escaped. We've got it in the car."

Both detectives were astounded at this turn of events. It was a moment or two before either one responded; when they did, it way Kelly who spoke first.

"Well, I guess now it's our turn to make sure he stays a resident of the state, either above or below the ground. Makes no mind to me," said Kelly.

"I agree with you there," Rick chimed in. "Do we know where he is?"

"Not yet, but Bob's working on that right now," Andy informed the two.

Back in their car, Bob was continuing his interrogation of Joey.

"I want a location where it will be easy for us to pick him up when he shows."

Joey thought for a moment then said to Bob, "You bring me over to our apartment in the University District. He feels pretty safe coming there because no one is supposed to know that we're connected. I'll call him and tell him everything went down ok. Then I'll tell him that I've got shit we can score. He'll show up for that, no matter what."

"I hope for your sake, and for Patti's, that you're right."

"I'm right, man, he'll be there."

Bob left Joey handcuffed in the back seat of his car and got out to talk to the other detectives gathered around the van. He filled them in on his conversation with Joey and his agreement to contact Hardy and set him up outside of his apartment in the University District. After a few minutes the men dispersed and headed to their cars. Sgt. Reed grabbed Bob before he returned to his car.

"Mind if you take along another rider?"

"Sure, Jake, the more the merrier."

"You need my men?"

"As a matter of fact, I was hoping you would offer."

"Say no more!"

Bob got back into his car with Andy and waited while Reed walked over to Seward and Benson. He spoke briefly with both men and then returned to Bob's car. Seward and Benson hustled Patti and her son out of the back seat of Reed's car and into the rear seat of the marked patrol unit at the scene. They asked the uniformed officer to deliver them to the precinct and place them in the holding cell and remain with them until they returned. They were not to be allowed to use the phone. Then, returning to their own car, they turned around and followed the caravan to the University District.

Chapter 67

The four units pulled up to the curb about two blocks north of NE 55th and 15th NE. Andy unhooked Joey's cuffs and let him out of the back seat.

Before he got out to the car, Bob leaned over and reminded him, "Remember, Joey, everything relies on your performance. You screw us over and the deal's off about Patti and the kids."

"I remember, man. I'll be back." Joey got out of the car and ran about a half a block to a little run-down apartment complex on the east side of the street. He unlocked the door and when he entered, went straight to the phone on the kitchen counter. He pulled out a pocket-sized brown address book from the drawer beneath the phone and dialed a number he retrieved from the back of the book.

The phone rang twice before Tucker picked it up.

"This is Joey; is he there?"

"Hold on, I'll get him."

Joey heard Tucker's muffled voice call for Hardy.

"Yeah. I was hoping it would be you. Is everything alright?" Nodding his head as the caller spoke, he replied, "Where should I meet you? And what time?" He paused and thought for a moment. "No, let's meet somewhere else; too many cops up there. Hold on." He placed his hand over the receiver and turned to Tucker.

"Where's a safe place up on Aurora that you know of?"

Without hesitation he answered, "'Frank's on 50th and Aurora."

"You know where Frank's on 50th and Aurora is?" He waited for a reply then said, "I'll be there, just make sure that you are."

Joey heard the phone click on the other end and the line went dead. His brain raced as he realized that now Johnny was determining the turf and not him. This could be dangerous. But hell, that wasn't his problem. The cops made a deal with him to set Hardy up, not actually catch him. That was their problem now. Joey raced out of the apartment and down the street back toward DeNucci's car. When he reached the car, he was out of breath and gasping for air.

"Settle down, Joey. Is he on his way?"

"Yeah, man." He stopped to catch his breath. "He's on his way, but not here."

"What do you mean, Joey? Are you trying to screw us?"

"No, man, I swear. He didn't want to meet here. He thinks there are too many cops drivin' through the area."

After he said that, he realized what it sounded like and immediately backtracked.

"I didn't tell him anything. It was his idea. He wants to meet up on Aurora at Frank's Market at 50th. Say's it's safer there. You know where it is?"

"We know where it is, Joey. You better not be bullshittin' us, you hear. 'Cause we can make it awfully uncomfortable for you and your family if you are."

"No way, man! I swear. He'll be there."

Andy picked up the radio and contacted Seward and Benson. He asked them to take off first and check out the market. Then they would meet just south of the market, on the east side of Aurora in the parking lot of a motel when they were done. Bob signaled Kelly, alone in his car, and Rick and his partner in their car, to meet them. Bob asked Kelly to call for a marked unit to hold on to Joey until they were sure they weren't being double-crossed. When the patrol car arrived, they placed Joey in the back.

"We'll call you when we're done to let you know about Patti," Bob told Joey as the uniformed officer placed him in the rear seat of his cruiser.

While he sat in the back of the patrol car, he mulled over what he was going to do *if* Johnny got out of this one.

Seward and Benson crossed the University District toward Aurora Avenue, When they reached Frank's Market, Seward pulled their black unmarked 1977 Camaro into the parking lot where it disappeared among a dozen or so cars already parked there. Each officer lit up a cigarette and assessed the area. They saw no sign of their suspect either in the lot or around the market. After about fifteen minutes, Benson got out and walked into the market to look around. He was in the market about two minutes when the Oldsmobile containing Tucker and Hardy pulled into the parking lot four spaces north of the Camaro. Hardy got out of the car and walked into the market where he stood at the counter next to Benson and bought a pack of cigarettes. When he walked out of the market, Benson was right behind him. Benson got back into the Camaro with Seward and they pulled out of the lot. A few minutes later they rendezvoused with the other officers in the parking lot of a little fleabag motel south of the market.

"Did you see anything?" Andy posed.

"Hell, yes," Benson replied. "He's there, with another guy."

"There in a green Oldsmobile," Seward chimed in.

Bob and Andy gathered everyone around the hood of their car as they went over the plan they devised on the way to the motel. The plan, which was elaborate for being put together on the go, detailed everyone's responsibility and position they would take to ensure the safety of all the officers during the arrest. Of course, what all of them should have remembered but did not was that Murphy was about to raised his ugly head once again.

According to Seward and Benson, the two suspects were seated in their car which was parked almost dead center in the parking lot. Seward would lead the way back into the lot since his vehicle was the least likely to be recognized as a police car. They would enter the lot from Aurora Avenue North and pull up behind the suspect vehicle, blocking it in its parking spot. Should things not go as planned and the suspects' vehicle gets away, Rick Reed and his partner would follow Seward's vehicle into the lot from Aurora and block off any possible entry to the main road. Bob and Andy along with Egan and Jake Reed, who had hopped in with Kelly, would turn off Aurora on North 49th, one block south of the market, and circle around. They would enter the east side of the lot where they would block off the exit while Bob and Andy swung around to the front of the suspect's car, careful not to get into any cross fire situation with Seward and Benson. Once they had sprung their trap there would be no place for Hardy to go. Or so they thought.

The cars left the motel parking lot in the order they would arrive at the market. Bob, Andy, Kelly and Jake turned east off of Aurora Ave one block south of the market just as planned. Seward and Benson were the first ones to reach the parking lot. As soon as they entered the lot, Seward brought the car to an immediate halt. The Olds was gone!

Bob and Andy, unaware of the dilemma the other officers were facing in the parking lot, continued their trek to the lot from the east side. As they approached the turn-off for the market their years of working together as a team paid one of its highest dividends. There was little time for either officer to react to what they encountered. There, parked on the street, directly south of the parking lot, was the Oldsmobile. Sitting on the hood of the car and smoking a cigarette was Johnny Hardy. Tucker, who appeared to be the more nervous of the two, was pacing on the sidewalk.

Bob was mid-sentence with Andy when he abruptly stopped speaking. When he caught sight of the two men and their car, his mouth suddenly became dry. Instantly he realized that everything had just gone to hell in a hand basket!

Things just got extremely dangerous, he thought to himself.

It wasn't necessary for either man to verbally communicate with the other. Andy was already removing his automatic from the holster beneath his jacket. Bob only hoped that Kelly and Jake picked up on it as quickly as they did. It was all improvisation from this point on.

He continued on down the street as though nothing unusual was about to happen. Quickly glancing in his rear view mirror, he could see the look of surprise on Jake Reed's face through the front windshield of his car. At least now he knew what he was going to do next would be no surprise to them.

What Johnny had in his favor was his instinct. As he sat on the hood of the car puffing on a cigarette, he really wasn't paying much attention to the road in front of him. Suddenly, his eye caught sight of a small glare caused by the reflection of the sun on the oncoming car's bumper. Reacting like a jaguar, he sprang from the hood of the car and would likely have gotten a pretty good head start on the officers, except for one thing. Murphy again! He crashed head first into Tucker, who, totally oblivious to the entire situation, grabbed onto Hardy as they tumbled to the ground in a heap.

As soon as Bob saw Hardy leap from the hood of the car, he accelerated toward him. Just before he reached the Oldsmobile, he put the car into a four-wheel drift and slid up in front of the car at a ninety-degree angle. Before they came to a halt, both officers were bailing out their respective sides, guns drawn. A second set of screeching tires told Bob that everyone else was on the same page as they were.

The first time Johnny had an inkling he was in trouble was when he hit the ground with Tucker below him. This was not how he figured on going out. With a burst of strength he propelled himself backward off Tucker, who still didn't realize what was happening, and rolled to a crouching position on the sidewalk. With little time to think, he reacted instinctively as the two men exited from what he was sure was the unmarked car he saw cruising up the street. He jumped to his feet, turned and scaled a three-foot hedge and chain-link fence that surrounded the small blue corner home behind him. When he hit the ground on the other side of the fence, he rolled over and immediately popped up running. A quick flash crossed his mind and he reached down and pulled a small automatic from the waistband of his jeans. For the first time in a long while, his instinct failed him. As he began to turn around and confront his pursuer, he never knew what happened, as the lights went out just before he hit the ground.

Chapter 68

As Bob bailed out of the driver's side door, he was groping for the handle of his automatic that was tucked into the shoulder holster under his coat. It felt like an eternity, but finally he managed to pull the gun from the holster. That's when he spotted Hardy jumping over the hedge into the front yard of the blue house. For a split second, Bob glanced at his partner and was sure that the second suspect, still on the sidewalk, was taken care of. With adrenaline pumping, Bob managed to hurdle over the hedge and chain-link fence in one leap and landed in the front yard of the blue house at a full run. A split second after touching the ground, Bob was confronted by a gun-wielding Johnny Hardy. Without a moment to gather his thoughts, it was Bob who acted instinctively. It was too late to do anything but run, so raising the gun in his right hand to absorb the shock, Bob, or should we say Bob's .9mm Smith and Wesson, ran head-first into Hardy skull. The bone-crunching impact was similar to that of an NFL quarterback being blind-sided by a 250-pound blitzing linebacker. The thud echoed across the front lawn of the residence and was enough to bring both Kelly Egan and Jake Reed to a complete halt just as they entered the fray.

Meanwhile, Andy pounced upon Tucker who was still dazed and lying on the sidewalk next to his car. The two men struggled but Andy, being the larger of the two, won easily. He also heard the thud on the other side of the hedge and wanted to get up and see what happened, but could not until he had subdued his suspect. By the time Tucker realized what was happening, he was handcuffed behind his back and was being lifted to an upright position by the larger man on top of him.

When he finally got Tucker to his feet he popped his head above the hedge to look for Bob.

Both men were on the ground and neither one was moving very fast. Finally, Bob, having the distinct advantage of landing on top of Hardy, managed to push himself up off the heap of garbage he had knocked to the ground. He picked up the small-caliber automatic on the ground next to Hardy and tucked it in his own waistband. As he began to brush himself off and reach for the handcuffs on his belt, Jake Reed rushed up and grabbed him by the arm to see if he was alright. Then looking down at the semiconscious Hardy, Reed chuckled, "And, Mr. Hardy, I see you've met our friends, Smith and Wesson?"

Jake took the cuffs from Bob and *gently*, using his size-thirteen shoe, rolled Hardy over on his stomach, knelt down and placed the cuffs on Hardy's wrists. Then, not quite as gingerly as he could have, he hoisted him up by the cuffs to a standing position. As he got to his feet, Hardy was wobbly and there was blood trickling from his mouth and nose. Bleary eyed and a bit incoherent, he looked over at Bob and asked, "I knew you were comin' sooner or later. I just didn't know when. How did you," he paused and thought for just a moment, "let me guess. Joey?

"Sorry, pal," Bob snickered, "professional secret." Then as an afterthought he said, "Besides, where you're going it's not going to matter any how."

"That son-of-a-bitch. He'll pay for this someday."

"You know, partner," Andy mocked as he peered over the hedge, "it works a lot better if you use that thing the way you were trained. You could have saved the state a lot of money." The Camaro with Seward and Benson pulled up next to the green Olds and when the two officers finally got out of their car Andy handed Tucker over to them.

"Sorry you guys missed all the fun. Next time we'll try and save some for you." He walked over to his partner and put his arm around his shoulder.

"You OK?"

"Yeah, I'll live. I'll be a little sore in the morning and I don't think I'll be giving the kids any piggy-back rides for a while, but I'll live." They both walked toward their car where Jake and Kelly were taking turns placing Hardy in the back seat.

"Oh, excuse me," Kelly feigned as Hardy's head seemed to bump the side of the door frame as he placed him in the car.

"Let me show you how to do that," Jake said as he removed Hardy from the back seat and once again managed to bump the side of his head as he eased him back in.

"Hey, you guys," Andy yelled, "aren't you going to leave anything for the courts to take a whack out of?"

"They tried that last time and look what it got us," Kelly yelled back. He pushed Jake Reed aside and reached back into the rear of the car to grab Hardy one more time. Hardy cringed as he anticipated the next wave of assaults by the two men outside the car. About halfway in Kelly stopped, stood up and said with disappointment, "Well, I guess you're right after all, although I hate to admit it." Then he slammed the door shut and walked back to his car.

"You know, Andy, I don't think I've hit some one that hard since my old football days."

"Yeah, well a Dick Butkus you're not, man. Next time if you're not going to pull the trigger, try throwing it. It'll save a lot of wear and tear on the body."

"No kidding. I've got to agree with you this time." After a few more steps he remembered that he should probably let their boss know what they had. "We probably better get a hold of Levi and let him know what we've got."

"Not so fast, Bob. Wait till I tell you the rest of the news. Me and ole Tucker over there, we had us a little chat. That is, he and Siggy," pointing to his .9mm Sig-Sauer automatic, "while he was resting on the sidewalk. And you'll never guess what ole Tucker told me. Seems our pal Hardy and his friends have spent the last few days over his house. He says they moved in their things downstairs, but he doesn't know what those things are. Now, if you had to guess, what do you think might be downstairs in ole Tucker's house?"

"Were does ole Tucker live?"

"He lives in the Mays Pond area in Snohomish County."

"You have an address?"

Andy reached into the breast pocket of his shirt and took out a small pad of white writing paper. When he read him the address, Bob almost choked.

"You're kidding, right?"

"No. Why?"

"You're not going to believe this but some of our best friends live right across the street from that address. In fact, the wife and kids and I were over there just the other night having dinner." Bob walked over to their car where Jake Reed was still standing and told him about the coincidence.

"It's a small world, isn't it?" said Jake as the two men rehashed the events that had just occurred. "So what's next?"

"Well, I was sort of hoping you would let us borrow two more of your men for a little while."

"Sure thing. What do you need them for?"

"Since we have to get the warrant in order, someone should be keeping an eye on Tucker's house just in case something goes down out there before we arrive."

"No problem. Church and Bello are at the precinct right now interviewing that redhead Grogen and Green picked up earlier. Give me an address and I'll give them a call and send them right over."

Bob was glad he could swing two more good officers from the pro active unit, especially these two. He gave Jake the address of his friends across the street from Tucker's house and told him that while he called the two officers he would call his friends and ask if the two men could use their house for the surveillance until the warrant arrived. Jake walked across the street to the phone booth at the market and called the precinct. He reached Church and gave him some details on the situation. Then he asked both men to go to the house across the street and keep an eye on the Tuckers' house until they could get a search warrant.

In the meantime Bob phone his friends in Mill Creek. After explaining the situation, they were more that willing to allow the two officers the use of their home for a while. After the phone call, Bob contacted Jake and let him know that the two officers would be expected.

Within ten minutes of the phone call all four cars were headed back to the Major Crimes Office in Seattle. Andy placed a radio call to Sgt. Levi prior to their departure from the arrest scene and he was waiting for them in the office when they arrived.

"It seems you two always have the knack of stepping in crap," he greeted them as the two officers escorted their prisoners into the bullpen.

"Yeah, well, you know us, boss, always rootin' around for something. Here's what we have." Andy filled Levi in on the arrest and Tucker's statements. On the way to the court house, Tucker had agreed to sign a consent to search his residence, but Levi felt that a search warrant would serve them better. So he and another detective sergeant began drafting the affidavit.

"What about the big guy? Is he saying anything?" asked Levi

"He wouldn't say shit if he had a mouth full," replied Andy.

"Well, let's get his ass over to the jail and then work on that search warrant. And remember, no phone privileges!"

Good news travels fast in the law enforcement community, so when the two men arrived upstairs at the jail, neither was surprised to see the booking room packed with most of the corrections officers on duty that night. Needless to say everyone there wanted their own piece of Hardy's hide for the murder of one of their own.

The jail commander met the men at the main door to the confinement area with a highly unorthodox request for them to accompany him and escort their prisoner personally to solitary where he would spend the remainder of his time with the county. It was not that he didn't trust his men to complete this task with the safety of the prisoner in mind, he explained to them, but he was well aware of the highly volatile emotions currently running through the ranks of his men and women and for the time, at least, didn't want to take any chances.

Bob and Andy reluctantly agreed to the request. Neither one of them like the idea of giving up their weapons and walking into a so-called "lion's den" unarmed, but they figured, what the hell, it might be fun seeing some of their old friends who were currently residing here. So, with the cuffs still fastened securely behind his back, the two officers walked their man up the cement ramps to the third tier of the jail where, with the assistance of the jail commander, he was placed in his new temporary home there at the jail.

Chapter 69

Before Johnny left the house in Mill Creek that afternoon, he woke Frank from a nap and told him to take whatever was left in the trunk of the blue Ford to the gold Mercury Cougar parked in the garage. Then he should call his buddy, Chuck, in Seattle and figure out how they could get rid of the Ford. It was almost two and a half hours after Johnny left that Linda came into Frank's room and pulled him out of his bed.

"Come on, you good-for-nothing. Johnny wanted us to unload the car. Let's get it done before he gets back. Karen and I will help you."

Frank pulled himself up from his bed and put on his shoes. He walked from the bedroom into the kitchen, opened the refrigerator and pulled out a beer. He twisted the top off and in three huge gulps drank it down. After a quick burp, he was ready to slip on his shirt and go out to the car.

While Karen opened the garage door with the inside controls, Linda and Frank went out the front door and walked over to the blue Ford. Frank got in and started it up. When the garage door was opened, he pulled the Ford in next to the gold Cougar but did not ask Karen to close the garage door. Instead, he got out and opened the trunk. Inside were several white canvas bank bags filled to the brim with cash collected from the Sea First Bank robbery that afternoon. Along with the cash were several weapons, some tape, chain and locks left over from previous robberies, an extra cowboy hat and some face makeup. While Frank lifted the canvas bags of money from the trunk, Karen and Linda helped with the rest. They were all so busy that none of them saw the two men walking up the driveway from the street.

Chapter 70

When Church and Bello pulled up into the driveway of DeNucci's friends on 173rd SE in Mays Pond, they got out of their car and walked up to the front door of the house as quickly as possible. The occupants of the house, being warned of their arrival in advance by Bob, were waiting when they knocked. Once they identified themselves, they were let in and led to the living room of the split-level where they could observe everything that went on at the house across the street. It was thirty minutes before they observed any movement at the house. A woman, later identified as Linda, came out of the house and checked the front seat of the blue Ford parked in the driveway. After about a minute of looking through the car, she headed back into the house. Not more than ten minutes later the two garage doors rolled up as two people, Linda and an unidentified man, came out the front door. A second woman walked out from the opened garage and met Linda and the unidentified man by the blue Ford. The man got into the Ford, started it up and pulled it into the garage. When he got out of the car, he didn't bother to close the garage door, but rather walked around to the back and opened up the trunk.

Neither officer could believe what they saw next.

"Well I'll be damned," Church whispered.

In broad daylight, with the garage doors wide open, Church and Bello observed the man as he lifted the first bag from the trunk. Church's mouth dropped. He could actually read the words Sea First Bank printed on the outside of the bag. As Bello continued to watch the man and two women transfer the contraband from the trunk of the blue Ford into the gold Cougar, Church placed a call downtown to DeNucci.

"Detective DeNucci."

"Hey Bob, it's Church. You're not going to believe what we're watching out here," he said excitedly then continued with his story. "Three people just came out of the house a few minutes ago. One of them, a guy kind of short and stocky, drove a blue Ford parked in the driveway into the opened garage where a second car was parked. Then he opened the trunk of the Ford and began unloading its contents into a Cougar that was parked next to it. Do you know what he's transferring from one car to the other?"

"No, but I'm sure you're going to tell me."

They're taking bank bags, filled to the brim with cash, out of one car and putting them into the trunk of the other. In broad daylight," Church repeated in disbelief. "Talk about a set of balls!"

"Are you sure they're bank bags?" With that statement, everyone in the bullpen became silent.

"Bob, I saw it with my own eyes. I read the words 'Sea First Bank' printed on the side."

"Well, you're on the scene. What does it look like to you?"

"Well, looks like they're planning to go somewhere."

Bob thought only for a moment. "Not anymore they're not. Take 'um down. Secure the house. We're on the way." Bob hung up and grabbed Andy. "Let's go, I'll fill you in on the way." Then turning to Levi before they left, he said, "We're headed for the house. Something's going down and Church and Bello are trying to get it under control. When you get the signed warrant let us know and meet us out there."

Church hung up and grabbed his partner. "Let's go. They're ours." Both men casually walked out of the front door of the residence and across the street. The three people at the house were so engrossed in moving the articles from one car to another they were totally taken by surprise when Church spoke.

"Police officers, everyone just stay where you are. No one make any unnecessary moves."

Frank, knowing the drill very well, froze at the trunk of the Cougar with Linda beside him. Karen, not realizing what was happening, continued to pick up items from the trunk of the Ford. Bello moved up alongside her with his gun drawn and grabbed her by the shoulder. Instantly she froze. Finally realizing what was happening, she collapsed to a seated position on the garage floor and began to cry. Linda and Frank joined her there as the two officers contained the three suspects and secured the house.

With the arrival of DeNucci and Anderson at the house and the arrest of the last three suspects, one of the most violent crime sprees in recent Northwest memories was now over. The sun was setting quickly, but the temperature was unusually warm for this late in the day. As the two men waited for Levi to arrive with the search warrant, they discussed the case with Church and Bello on the front lawn of the residence.

"So now what?" asked Church.

Bob checked his watch. "Well, first things first. We wait till the warrant arrives and then we see what our friends are hiding in the house."

"Speaking of what's hiding in the house," Church interrupted, "you know it was necessary for one of us to enter the house and make sure there were no more suspects inside."

"I figured you'd do something like that. Are we in for any surprises when we go in?" he asked.

"Surprises? Well, maybe a few. The place is packed with stuff, and if my nose is working properly, I'd say you've got more than you bargained for. If I were you, I would call the local sheriff's office and have them get some of their drug guys down here to check it out, 'cause I think you're going to have your hands full with the other stuff you find inside."

"Thanks for the heads up," Bob replied. "How's that sound to you A—" Bob turned to ask his partner a question but he had disappeared. "Now where did he go?" he mused. Then after a quick glance of the area he located the burly blonde in an adjoining yard. Bob smiled as he watched Andy jot down the phone number of a large-breasted blonde sitting crossed-legged on the front steps of the house next door. He deftly folded the small piece of paper and placed it in his shirt pocket.

Epilogue

At nine o'clock that evening, Sgt. Levi and several other Major Crimes Detectives arrived at the Noll residence and served a warrant sign by Superior Court Judge Johnson.

Everything at the house, now considered a crime scene, was recorded with photographs and sketches and accurate notes were taken.

"Physical evidence, when it is properly collected, marked and preserved, does not have memory lapses, cannot lie or be corrupted and cannot be impeached" (*Pilant*, 1992, p 42).

As a result of the search warrant served at the Noll residence, the safe house in Carnation, Ludnick's apartment and the storage locker in Edmonds, the police recovered over $35,000 in cash from the Sea First Bank robbery; over twenty-five stolen guns from the Sportees robbery; $40-$50,000 of assorted jewelry from the Jewel Box robbery; thousands of stolen drivers license blanks from the state of Oregon; a lock and some duct tape from Sears; several sawed-off shotguns; a stolen van; jewelry stolen during an armed robbery in Phoenix, Arizona; narcotics and narcotic paraphernalia and a mish-mash of stolen property belonging to burglary and larceny victims throughout the Northwest. An additional bonus for the detectives serving the warrant was the uncovering of a large marijuana-growing operation in the basement of the Noll residence. The detectives at the scene notified the Snohomish County Sheriff's Department of the find and their officers confiscated over four hundred plants in excess of three feet tall from an unfinished basement room in the Noll home.

Within months of the arrests, most of the defendants in the case were sentenced.

Johnny Hardy received two consecutive life terms in the state penitentiary at Walla Walla, Washington, for the murder of the Franklin J. Pierce and the Sears security guard.

Nora Chin plead guilty to the armed robberies of Sportees Gun Shop, the Jewel Box and the Raggamuffin, as well as accessory to murder in the murder of Franklin J. Pierce. She received a life sentence plus twenty years in the women's correctional facility at Purdy.

Frank Alanzo pled guilty to the Sea First Bank robbery as well as several other robberies and burglaries and received ten to fifteen years in the state penitentiary at Walla Walla.

Linda, his girlfriend, received five to ten years in the women's correctional facility at Purdy for her part in the armed robbery of the Sea First Bank.

Tucker and Karen Noll both received five years probation for their part in the Sea First Bank robbery. In addition, they were charged with possession with the intent to sell by Snohomish County Authorities and were given a deferred one-year sentence. After their arrests and charging and prior to their criminal trials, the Nolls attempted to sue King County for wrongful arrests. Judge John Callahan heard the case in King County Superior Court. After reviewing the evidence, Judge Callahan dismissed the case against the county.

John Ludnick and Susan Kearson turned State's evidence and were given immunity for their part in the bank robbery in turn for their testimony.

Jim Green was implicated in the death of the Sears security guard by a statement given by Frank Alanzo. He was arrested, and in return for his testimony against Hardy, was allowed to plead guilty to Manslaughter. He was sentenced to five years in Walla Walla, Washington.

Lorenzo Pena, who was implicated by Nora, left the area and headed back toward the East Coast. A warrant was issued for his arrest. His presence is unknown at this time.

Patti and Joey Mendosa. Patti was released from custody at the precinct on the same evening that Hardy was arrested. She returned to her apartment in the University District.

Joey, although not arrested the day of the robbery, was later charged in the robbery and shooting at the Lotus Blossom Restaurant. He and Patti left their children with her mother in Seattle and fled to Los Angeles where they intended to bring the children after they found a safe place to stay. Two months after arriving in Los Angeles, both were killed when Joey rolled their van while trying to elude the California Highway Patrol for a minor traffic violation.

Printed in the United States
70075LV00005B/1

9 781424 162024